SCIENCE

AP Smith

2000

GW00493872

SCIENCE

2000

BOOK TWO

Developed from *Science for the 70's* by

A. J. Mee, Patricia Boyd and David Ritchie

Heinemann Educational Books

Heinemann Educational Books Ltd
22 Bedford Square, London WC1B 3HH
LONDON EDINBURGH MELBOURNE AUCKLAND
HONG KONG SINGAPORE KUALA LUMPUR NEW DELHI
IBADAN NAIROBI JOHANNESBURG
EXETER (NH) KINGSTON PORT OF SPAIN

ISBN 0 435 57567 8
First published 1981
Reprinted 1982

British Library Cataloguing in Publication Data

Mee, A. J.
  Science 2000
  Book 2
  1. Science
  I. Title   II. Boyd, P.
  III. Ritchie, D.   IV. Science for the 70's
  500   Q161.2
ISBN 0-435-57567-8

Printed and bound in Great Britain by
Fakenham Press Limited, Fakenham, Norfolk

Preface

This book is the successor to *Science for the 70's*. The order of the Units of the original work has been retained, but there is a considerable amount of change within the Units, both in presentation and in new matter. There are also many new illustrations.

The book can be used in conjunction with the *New Science Worksheets* compiled by a working party set up by the Scottish Central Committee on Science, and published by Heinemann Educational Books, but it can, of course, be used independently.

It has not been felt necessary to provide a Teacher's Guide to the new book, such as accompanied *Science for the 70's*, because particularly useful Guides have been published in connection with the *New Science Worksheets* (*Scottish Integrated Science Teacher's Guides, Sections 1–8* and *Sections 9–15*, published by Heinemann Educational Books). These should provide all the information a teacher requires to present the course successfully.

We are much indebted to many people who were consulted about, and gave advice on, the material in this book; it is not possible to name them all. We would however give special thanks to Graham Taylor and Debbie Ganz, of Heinemann Educational Books, who exercised their considerable expertise in the production of the book, and to Helen Baird who gave much help in checking the proofs and compiling the index.

A. J. Mee
P. Boyd
D. Ritchie
September 1981

Contents

Acknowledgements

Acknowledgement is due to the following for permission to reproduce photographs in the text:

Ardea Photographics, 9.9 (b) woodmouse
Aerofilms, 12.3, 12.4
Heather Angel, 12.36, 13.44 (spider, crab, prawn)
Barnaby's Picture Library, 9.19 (a) (b), 9.26 (a) (b), 9.29, 9.31 (a), 13.1, 14.6
Besam, 9.33 (b) automatic doors
Bell Lines, 13.2
Biophotos, 11.31
Blue Circle, 12.19
Anne Bolt, 9.31 (b) (c)
British Gas, 9.32 (c), 12.24
British Museum, 13.43, 13.44
British Railways Board, 9.33 (a)
British Steel, 12.15, 12.16
Brooker & How Ltd, 9.19 (b)
BSR (Housewares) Ltd, 9.5 (c) (d)
Colorsport, 13.1 (c)
Costain, 13.2 (bottom)
Crittall Warmlife Ltd, 9.7 (d)
Stephen Dalton, 13.44 centipede, butterfly, locust, fly
Electricity Council, 9.32 (a), 15.7
Anne Fisher, 9.5 (a), 13.12
The Glasshouse, 12.21

Griffin & George Ltd, 14.10
Ian Griffiths – Title page
ICI Ltd, 9.7 (a)
Institute of Geological Sciences (Crown Copyright), 12.1, 12.6, 12.7, 12.8, 12.9
Lec Refrigeration Ltd, 9.27
London Brick Company, 12.18 (a) (b) (c) (d) (e) (f)
Middlemore's (Coventry), 13.13
National Portrait Gallery, 13.25 (Newton)
National Coal Board, 9.32 (b), 12.23
NASA – Back cover
Natural History Photographic, 13.45, 13.46, 13.47
Oxfam, 14.3
Pilkingtons, 12.20
Picturepoint, 9.9 (a) (c), 9.31 (d), 12.17, 14.1
Paul Popper, 13.1 (c) (bottom)
Ginge Raadvad, 13.1 (b)
Radio Times Hulton Picture Library, 15.17
Royal Aircraft Establishment, 13.18
Royal Postgraduate Medical School (Dr S. M. Lewis), 14.21 (a) (b)
Ted Roose & Partners Ltd, 9.5 (b)
Rentokil Labs Ltd, 9.7 (b) (c)
Shell, 12.25, 12.26, 12.27

UNIT 9

Heat flow

9.1 PARTICLES AND ENERGY

In Unit 3 of Book 1 you were introduced to many different forms of energy, one of which was **heat.** You are now going to find out more about heat. It is a very important form of energy. You will remember that we cannot afford to waste heat energy, and one of the things you will have to think about in this Unit is how we can try to save it.

Can you make a list of some of the ways in which heat is important to us? You might put into your list the ways in which houses and schools are heated, and also any industries that need heat to make things.

Now make a list of our sources of heat, including the various **fossil fuels** which we use.

Before starting the experiments it will help if you can remember what you learned in Unit 4 about matter; and how matter can exist in different states, called the **solid**, **liquid**, and **gaseous states**.

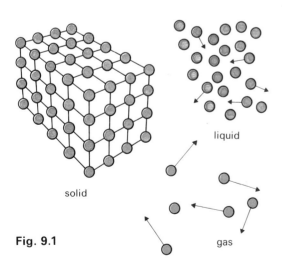

Fig. 9.1

solid

liquid

gas

The particles in solids, either atoms or molecules, are arranged in ranks and files and make a definite pattern. They shake, or 'vibrate', when given heat energy.

In a liquid the particles are about as far apart as in a solid, but they are not arranged in ranks and files. They are 'all over the place'! They move more freely than the particles of a solid.

Particles of a gas are spaced further apart than those in a liquid. They can move about more easily, and more quickly too. They usually move with something like the speed of a rifle bullet.

9.2 HOW HEAT TRAVELS

You are now going to find out how heat energy travels in different substances. The ideas about particles will help to explain what happens.

Experiment 9.1
Heating a metal rod

Hold the metal rod at one end and heat the other end in a Bunsen flame (Fig. 9.2). What do you feel happening to your fingers after a while?

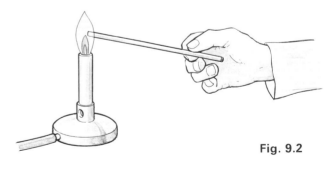

Fig. 9.2

What do you think is happening in the rod?

The heat energy has travelled along the rod from the hot flame to your cooler fingers. It must have been passed on from one end of the rod to the other.

Does our particle theory explain this? When the rod is heated what will the particles do? As they are in the solid state they are held in place and vibrate. If you go on supplying energy to them they vibrate more and more. They move so far from side to side that they affect their neighbours, and these particles in turn will vibrate more. In this way the energy will pass along the metal from the hot end of the rod to the cold end. This method of transferring heat from one particle to another is called **conduction.**

Experiment 9.2
Comparing different rods

You are going to find out whether heat is conducted at the same speed by two different metals, copper and iron. How can you be sure that you are comparing them fairly? If one rod was shorter than the other do you think the heat would get to the other end of the short rod sooner? Would it make any difference if one rod was thinner?

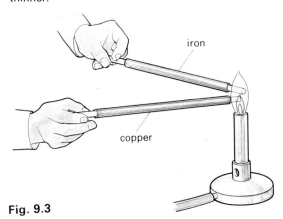

iron

copper

Fig. 9.3

The copper and iron rods you will use have been coated with wax. At exactly the same time place one end of each of the rods in a Bunsen flame. If you are working with a partner you could each hold one. Carefully watch what happens to the wax as the heat flows along the rods. Along which rod is the wax melting faster?

Both metals have **conducted** the heat, and so we say they are both **conductors** of heat. Which metal is the better conductor?

With help from other people in your class it would be possible to make a list of lots of metals, starting with the best conductors and finishing with the worst. To do this you would have to have enough rods of the different metals which were all the same length and thickness.

Copper and aluminium are the best conductors. Can you think of reasons why modern electric 'irons' are not made of iron any more, but are mainly aluminium?

Experiment 9.3
Comparing the rates at which heat is conducted in plastic and metal spoons

For this experiment you will need plastic and metal spoons which are as nearly the same size as possible. You will also need some very hot water. Perhaps you could heat the water in an electric kettle until it is nearly boiling. **Very carefully** pour some of this water into a beaker. Now hold the metal and plastic spoons in the

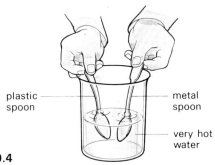

plastic spoon

metal spoon

very hot water

Fig. 9.4

hot water, as shown in Fig. 9.4. It is best if one person uses both hands to do this. Why? Keep the spoons in the hot water for a few minutes. Which spoon handle feels hot first?

The plastic has not conducted the heat to your fingers as well as the metal has. You have found that plastic is a poor conductor of heat. It is sometimes called a **heat insulator**. Do you remember that poor conductors of electricity are called electrical insulators?

The things in these pictures all use good conductors of heat. Why do you think it is sensible to have plastic handles?

(a) A soldering iron. How does it work?

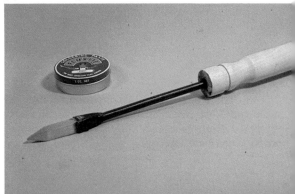

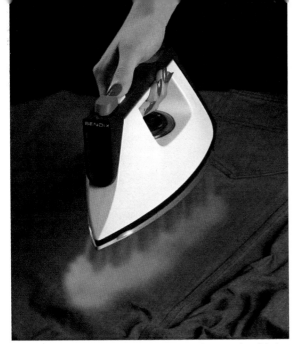

(b) An electric iron. Give reasons why much of it is made of plastics.

(c) An electric kettle.

(d) What is each part of this saucepan made of? Why?

Fig. 9.5

Experiment 9.4
Is water a good conductor of heat?

In this experiment, and in some others which follow, you will be using thermometers again. Remember: **always treat them carefully.**

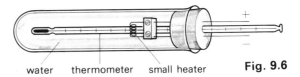

water   thermometer   small heater   **Fig. 9.6**

You will use the apparatus shown in Fig. 9.6. It will already have been set up for you. The test-tube is filled with water. First read the temperature on the thermometer and write this reading down. Now connect the terminals marked + and − to your power pack and adjust the voltage to 6 volts. Note the time and switch on the small heater. Leave it on for exactly two minutes. Then switch it off and read the temperature again. Has it changed at all?

If the thermometer reading has not changed what does this mean? Has any heat travelled from the hot wire through the water to the thermometer bulb?

From this experiment you will have seen that water is a poor conductor of heat. This may surprise you as you know that we can make water hot. However, when water is heated the heat does not travel through it by conduction. You will find out more about this later.

Experiment 9.5
Is air a good conductor of heat?

The apparatus for this experiment is very similar to that used in the last experiment, but this time the test-tube is full of air. Notice that there is an extra hole in the stopper. Make sure that this hole does not get blocked during the experiment, otherwise the stopper might fly off, or the test-tube might shatter. Do you know why?

Clamp the test-tube as it was in the last experiment. Note down the reading on the thermometer. Now connect the + and − terminals to the power pack. Set the voltage to 6 volts and switch on the heater for exactly two minutes. Then switch it off and read the thermometer once more. Has the temperature changed? If it has not, has any heat travelled from the hot wire to the bulb of the thermometer?

You have found that air is also a bad conductor of heat. In fact, air is a very important heat insulator.

9.3 SOME USES OF AIR AS AN INSULATOR

Fuels and other sources of heat are very expensive. Also the sources of energy in the world are being used up and we must do our best not to waste them. So when we have changed energy into heat we try not to let it escape.

The pictures in Fig. 9.7 show some of the ways we can insulate parts of our homes. All the insulating materials have one thing in common. Can you spot what this is? They all contain spaces – some large, some small – filled with air.

The hot water storage tank in your house is probably 'lagged' to stop it from losing heat. Find out where the tank is and what the lagging is made of. It may be glass fibre, or perhaps some other fibrous material. Air is trapped between the fibres. The material itself is a bad conductor, and so is the air.

What do you use to keep a pot of tea hot? What is it made of, and what will this contain?

Of course, the materials you have just been reading about, which are insulators and prevent heat escaping, will also stop heat from getting in. If you defrost the refrigerator or freezer you may be told to take any frozen foods out and wrap them in layers of newspaper until the defrosting is finished. How does the newspaper help to keep the food from thawing?

Fig. 9.7 Insulation of (a) cavity walls, (b) roof, and (c) pipes. What is the similarity between the various insulating materials used? (d) How does double glazing help keep the house warm?

(b)

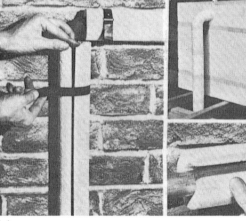

(c)

(a)

(d)

A home experiment

It is not always necessary to use complicated apparatus in a laboratory to do experiments. Here is something you can try at home. Get a metal or 'tin' mug and an expanded polystyrene or foam drinking cup. Make some hot tea or coffee and pour equal amounts into each container. Put these on a metal surface—perhaps a metal draining board or something like that. Wait for about 7 or 8 minutes. Now taste each drink in turn. In which container is the drink hotter? Why is this?

9.4 KEEPING WARM

At home and in factories fuels are burned to make heat. We and other animals 'burn' up food as fuel in our bodies to keep ourselves warm. Do you remember what your normal body temperature is? Is it higher than the usual temperature of the air?

Old people who cannot afford to buy enough fuel for their homes and food for their bodies in winter may become very ill. They become very cold and their body temperature falls. Do you know what we call this condition?

Climbers lost in a blizzard may also suffer from this loss of heat, which is called hypothermia. They can sometimes avoid it by getting inside a large plastic bag, keeping their heads out, of course. How does this help to keep them warm?

Animals have different coverings to keep them warm. They may be covered with fur, hair, feathers, or wool. Now you will do an experiment to find out how good these coverings are at stopping animals from losing heat.

You cannot, of course, use the animals themselves for these experiments so you will use flasks instead!

Experiment 9.6
How good are felt, fur, and feathers as insulators?

You need four flasks for this experiment. They must all be the same size. Fill one of them with warm water and empty it into an electric kettle. Do this twice more so that you will have enough hot water to fill each flask about three-quarters full. Wrap fur round one flask, felt (or cotton wool, which will represent wool) round another, feathers round the third, and leave the fourth without any covering.

Heat the water in an electric kettle until it is almost boiling. Take the stoppers with their thermometers out of the flasks and put them in a safe place where they will not roll away. Carefully clamp each of the flasks with their bottoms about 3 or 4 cm above the base of each stand. Then carefully fill each flask with the very hot water to the same level, as shown in the diagram. Take great care not to let the water spill onto the coverings of the flasks or onto your fingers. Holding the stoppers between finger and thumb, replace them and the thermometers into the flasks. Give each stopper a gentle twist to make sure it is firm. Read the temperature on each thermometer and write down the readings in a table like the one below.

Time (minutes)	Flask A	Flask B	Flask C	Flask D
0 20				

After 20 minutes take the thermometer readings again and enter them in the table.

Which flask shows the smallest drop in temperature? Are the coverings better insulators than nothing at all?

Fig. 9.8

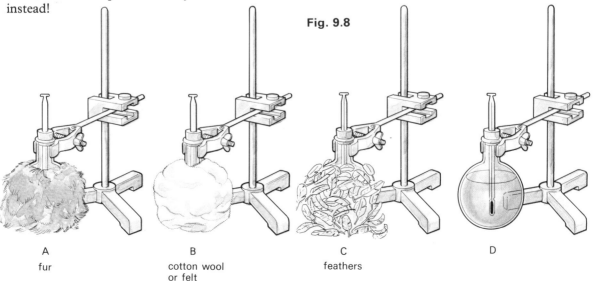

A	B	C	D
fur	cotton wool or felt	feathers	

Felt, fur, and feathers have lots of trapped air between the fibres, and it is because this air is a bad conductor of heat that animals do not lose too much heat during the winter.

If you have a pet cat or dog, what have you noticed happening to its coat during the winter? The thicker coat your pet grows prevents it losing heat because the hairs trap extra pockets of air. On a cold day you might think that the small birds in your garden have suddenly become fat. Has this really happened? What is the explanation? The birds have ruffled up their feathers to trap more air to insulate them from the cold.

Fig. 9.9 How are these animals insulated against the cold?

(a)

(b)

9.5 COOLING DOWN

Experiment 9.7
A cooling curve

Carefully fill a beaker with hot water. Take the temperature of the water, and take it again each minute, using a stop-clock to tell you the time.

Fig. 9.10

hot water   stop clock

(c)

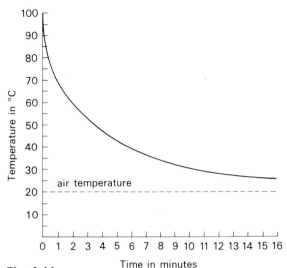

Fig. 9.11

Note the temperatures in a table. Then draw a graph on squared paper with the temperature on the vertical axis and the time on the horizontal axis. Join up all the points with a smooth curve. You will probably get a curve like the one in Fig. 9.11.

In your maths class you have probably had practice in drawing graphs and getting information from them. See if you can answer the following questions about the graph in Fig. 9.11.
(a) What was the temperature of the water at the beginning of the experiment (zero time)?
(b) What was the temperature after one minute?
(c) By how much did the temperature fall during this first minute?
(d) Did the temperature fall by this amount every minute?
(e) Does the rate at which the water cools get greater or smaller as time goes on?
(f) Although the graph stops after 16 minutes, what do you think the final temperature of the water would be if you had waited long enough?
(g) Where has all the heat that was in the hot water gone?

Experiment 9.8
More cooling curves

You need two metal cylinders with holes drilled down the middle into which thermometers can be put. The cylinders must be the same. Put them into a beaker and carefully pour boiling water over them until the level of the water is about 1 cm from the top of the cylinders.

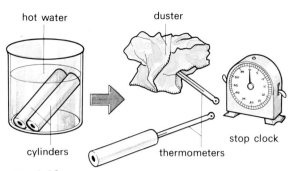

Fig. 9.12

After they have been in the very hot water for about 3 minutes carefully pour off the water and pick out the cylinders. (They will be very hot, so you will need to use a holder of some kind.) Insert a thermometer in each hole. Cover one of the cylinders with an insulating material – perhaps some cotton wool, or a duster, or you could put a heap of plastic chips round it. Leave the other cylinder uncovered in the air. Take the readings of the thermometers every minute for about 20 minutes and make a note of the results in a table like the one below.

Time (minutes)	Temperature of covered cylinder	Temperature of uncovered cylinder
0 1 2		

Draw graphs of your results on the same axes, with temperature on the vertical axis and time on the horizontal one. If you mark the points for the covered cylinder with crosses and those for the uncovered cylinder with circles you will be able to tell which set of results is which. Join up the crosses and then the circles with smooth curves to give two cooling curves.

For which cylinder has the temperature fallen quicker?

Is the rate of cooling the same at all parts of the graphs? (That is, does the temperature in, for example, the first three minutes fall faster or slower than during the second three minutes, or any other three minute interval you like to take, or is the temperature change the same in all intervals of three minutes?)

For which cylinder is the average rate of cooling greater?

Would it be possible to use this kind of experiment to compare the worth of different insulators? What would you have to do to make sure that each insulating material was being compared fairly?

9.6 A SECOND WAY IN WHICH HEAT TRAVELS

Experiment 9.9
How does heat travel in water if it is a poor conductor?

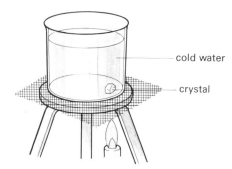

Fig. 9.13

Put a single crystal of potassium permanganate at the bottom of a beaker of cold water, as near to one edge as possible. Begin to heat the water with a small Bunsen flame directly underneath the crystal. (Remember that the outside of the beaker must be dry before you start heating.)

What do you notice about the direction in which the coloured liquid moves? What happens when it gets to the top? Will it be only the particles of the crystal which are moving in this way?

Although you cannot see the water particles they must be moving in the same way as the permanganate ones. Can we explain why the particles move in this direction? Think about what happens to the spacing of the particles in a liquid as it is heated. As the particles get more energy they will spread out and take up more space. So in any particular volume of hot liquid (say $1\ cm^3$) there will be fewer particles than in $1\ cm^3$ of cold liquid, and this hot $1\ cm^3$ will weigh less than the cold liquid. This makes the hot liquid float to the top in the beaker. It is less dense than the colder liquid.

When the hot liquid gets to the top it meets the colder air, and becomes cooler again as it loses some of its heat energy. This makes the particles crowd closer together again, and so they sink down.

You will see that the hot liquid, when it rises to the top, takes its heat with it. This, then, is another way in which heat energy can be taken from one place to another. It can be carried by the particles themselves instead of being handed on from one particle to the next.

This effect of a liquid rising when heated and sinking when cooled, so that the liquid circulates, is called **convection**.

Why can convection not take place in a solid? Can it take place in a gas?

Experiment 9.10
How does heat travel in air which is a bad conductor?

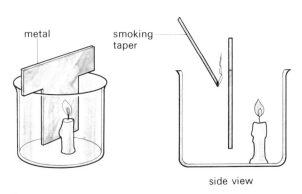

Fig. 9.14

Light the candle and hold a smouldering taper at the top of the beaker as shown in Fig. 9.14. What do you see happening to the smoke from the taper? You will notice that the smoke is drawn down the one side of the partition and rises up on the other side where the flame of the candle is. The smoke shows you the direction in which the air particles are moving. The candle flame is heating the air, and the hot air rises just as the heated water did in the last experiment.

The air particles also spread out when they are heated. They are then less closely packed and they float upwards. Here the heat is travelling in air in the same way it did in water in the last experiment – by convection. The moving particles of smoke are evidence of what we call **convection currents.**

You will remember that both liquids and gases are called fluids because they flow easily. We can therefore say that heat can travel by convection in fluids, but not in solids.

Experiment 9.11
Comparing conduction and convection in water

The apparatus is set up as shown in Fig. 9.15.

Clamp the test-tube near its mouth, but not too tightly, or you will crack the glass. Make sure that the tube is held straight up and down. Take the temperature of the cold water in the tube. Now connect the + and − terminals to the power pack. Adjust the voltage to 6 volts and switch it on for 1 minute. Now switch off the current and read the thermometer. Has the temperature changed at all? If not, why not?

This experiment is similar to Experiment 9.4, but you are doing it here as a **control**. Next you are going to repeat the experiment with only one thing changed, and see what happens then.

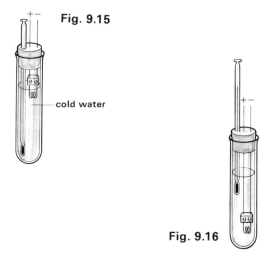

Fig. 9.15

cold water

Fig. 9.16

Fill the test-tube with fresh cold water as before, but this time move the thermometer and heater to the new positions shown in Fig. 9.16. Make sure that the thermometer bulb is near the surface of the water and the heater is at the bottom. As before, take the temperature of the water, switch on the power pack using 6 volts for 1 minute only, and then take the temperature again.

The only difference between this experiment and the control experiment is in the position of the thermometer and the heater. Is there any difference in the results? Are the thermometer readings different this time? You should find that they are. What has carried the heat up to the thermometer?

What does the experiment tell us about conduction and convection in water?

Experiment 9.12

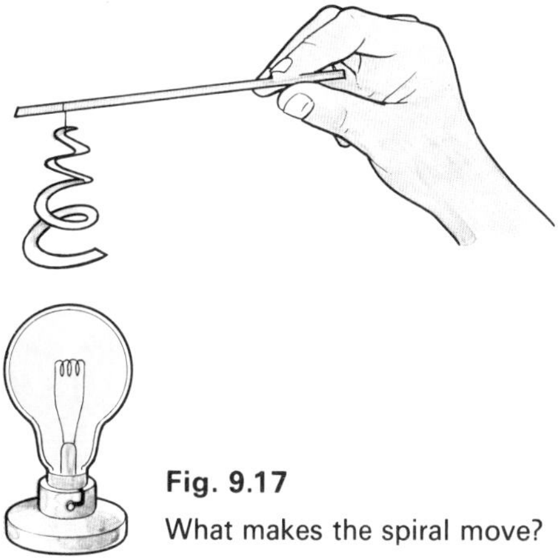

Fig. 9.17

What makes the spiral move?

Cut a spiral from a circular piece of stiff paper about 10 cm in diameter. Make a large knot in a piece of thread and with a needle push the thread through a hole in the centre of the spiral. Now tie the thread to a rod or pencil. Switch on the lamp and hold the spiral above it. What happens? What makes the spiral spin round?

If you are not sure, hold the rod with the spiral above your head and blow upwards.

What does this show about the air heated by the lamp?

Experiment 9.13

Make a paper box out of a sheet of paper about 20 cm square. You can make it like the one in the diagram by using paper clips. If you or your friends have ever done ORIGAMI (Japanese paper folding), you will know that it is quite easy to make one without clips. The paper must not be torn or folded over too hard, or it might leak.

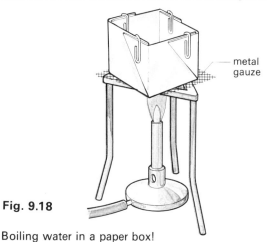

metal gauze

Fig. 9.18

Boiling water in a paper box!

Put your box on a piece of wire gauze on a tripod stand. Now pour cold water into the box to a depth of about 1 cm. Light the Bunsen and adjust it to give a small flame. Put the Bunsen under the tripod.

If you are patient you may see tiny bubbles appear at the bottom of the water and steam might rise. This will show that the water is boiling in the box.

In this experiment the wire gauze, which is a good conductor, spreads out the heat from the flame. But why does the paper not burn? What is taking away the heat from the paper bottom of the box?

9.7 CONVECTION CURRENTS IN AIR AND WATER

These pictures show some examples of convection currents in our everyday life.

Fig. 9.19 (a) What makes the balloon go up?

Fig. 9.19 (b) Explain how a convector heater like one of these can warm up a large room.

Fig. 9.19 (c) Why does the glider sometimes make a sudden upward flight?

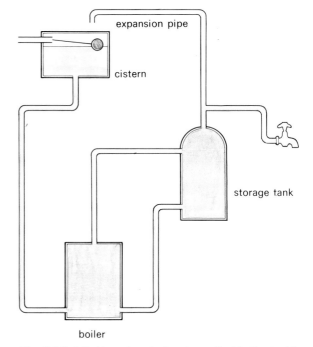

Fig. 9.19 (d) How does hot water collect in the tank?

Fig. 9.19 (e) The diagram shows how the breeze blows at the seaside during a warm day. Can you puzzle out which way it will blow at night?

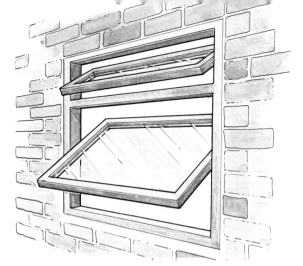

Fig. 9.19 (f) The room is warm. Which way will air flow into the room—through the bottom or the top of the open window?

9.8 A THIRD WAY IN WHICH HEAT TRAVELS

In Book 1, Unit 3 you were told about a third way in which heat can travel. There we spoke about 'infra red' energy which travels in invisible waves. This is also called 'radiant' energy, or sometimes **radiation**. Heat energy travels to us from the Sun across empty space by radiation. The Sun is about 148 million kilometres (93 million miles) away from us, but it takes only 8 minutes 20 seconds for the heat from it to reach us.

Experiment 9.14
Using a light bulb as a miniature Sun

Hold the thermometer about 10 cm from the lamp as shown in Fig. 9.20. Note the reading on the thermometer. Then switch on the lamp for a few minutes. What do you notice happening to the thermometer reading? If the reading has gone up, can the heat from the lamp have travelled to the thermometer by conduction? Why not? Can it have travelled to the thermometer by convection? Why not?

Remember that we have already found that the air between the lamp and thermometer is a bad conductor of heat, and that heated air in a convection current rises upwards and not sideways.

The heat must have travelled from the lamp to the bulb by the only other method – **radiation**.

Switch on the lamp again and notice the temperature rise. Now put quite a small object, like a half pence piece, in front of the thermometer bulb. What happens to the reading?

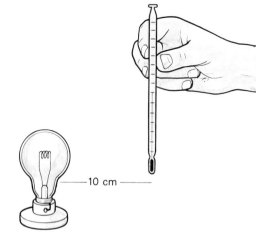

Fig. 9.20

The coin, or similar object, must have stopped the heat radiation getting to the thermometer bulb. It has also made a shadow on the thermometer bulb. Heat rays, just like light, travel in straight lines.

Experiment 9.15
Does colour affect the amount of heat radiated by a hot object?

You will need two flasks of the same size. One is painted black on the outside. The other is painted with aluminium paint to make it shiny.

Fill the two flasks with boiling water and fit the stoppers and thermometers carefully. Note down the readings on the thermometers.

Take the temperatures again after about 10 minutes. In which flask has the temperature fallen faster? From which flask has the heat radiated away faster?

Fig. 9.21

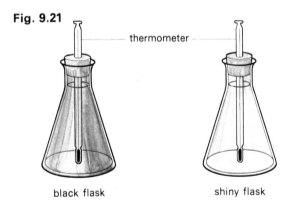

thermometer

black flask   shiny flask

. Experiment 9.16
Does colour affect the amount of heat absorbed by a cold object?

In this experiment the flasks, shown in Fig. 9.22, are full of air. Note down the temperatures on the thermometers and then switch on the heater for about two

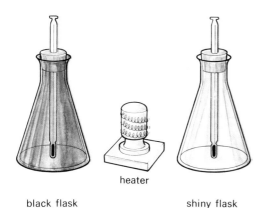

heater

black flask   shiny flask

Fig. 9.22

minutes. Be careful not to let anything touch the heater when it is on. Not only can it burn badly, it can give an electric shock as well. If you do not wish to use a heater you can use a light bulb, but then the experiment takes longer.

When the time is up take the temperatures again. In which flask has the temperature risen more? Which one has absorbed more heat energy?

What have you noticed as a result of the last two experiments? In both experiments the black flask has firstly, radiated heat better, and secondly, absorbed heat better than the shiny glass flask. The shiny glass surface has acted like a mirror, and in the last experiment it probably reflected back the radiant heat.

Experiment 9.17
Heat passing through a vacuum

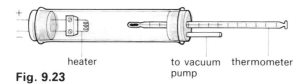

heater   to vacuum   thermometer
                      pump

Fig. 9.23

Set up the apparatus as shown in Fig. 9.23. Read the thermometer with air in the tube and the heater off. Now switch the heater on until it is red hot. Read the temperature again after exactly two minutes and note any change. Now switch the heater off. Connect the tube to a vacuum pump. Turn it on and keep it working for long enough to make sure that a reasonably good vacuum is produced in the tube.

Switch on the heater again so that it is red hot. After 2 minutes note any rise in temperature.

Is there much difference between the two increases in temperature? '

Obviously heat can travel through a vacuum by radiation.

Experiment 9.18
The vacuum flask

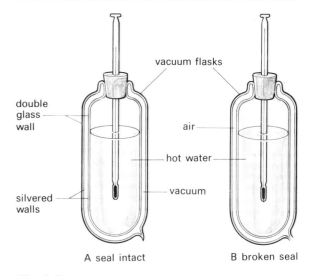

vacuum flasks

double
glass
wall

air

hot water

silvered
walls

vacuum

A seal intact   B broken seal

Fig. 9.24

You will have two flasks. One of them is perfect. The other has had the seal broken so that there is air between the walls of the flask instead of a vacuum.

Fill each flask with equal volumes of nearly boiling water from an electric kettle and stopper each one as shown in the diagram. Note the temperature on each thermometer at intervals of 1 minute for 15 minutes. Which flask has lost its heat quicker?

Both flasks have shiny silver walls. Which method of heat flow do these shiny walls prevent in each flask?

Both flasks are made of glass. Glass is not a good conductor, so heat will not be lost by conduction. But one flask has air between the walls. Do you think heat is more likely to travel through this air from the hot contents by conduction or convection? Is this why the damaged flask cooled more quickly?

Although nowadays we usually use a vacuum flask to prevent a hot liquid from cooling down, this type of flask was invented by a Scottish scientist, Sir James Dewar, to keep a cold liquid from warming up.

Experiment 9.19
More effects of colour

Fig. 9.25

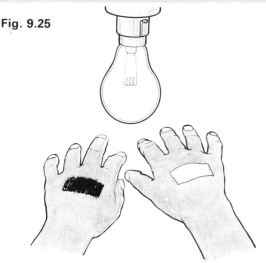

Fig. 9.27 Why is the back of the refrigerator silvered, the pipes black, and the sides white?

Paint an area about 4 to 5 cm square on the back of one hand with water-based white paint. Paint an area the same size on the back of your other hand with water-based black paint. This paint washes off easily. If you do not have any paint of this kind use black foil on one hand and silver foil on the other. Now hold the backs of both hands together under a lit light bulb for about 10 seconds. Which hand becomes hotter? Can you remember why?

This experiment shows us once again that a black surface absorbs radiant heat better than a shiny or white surface.

Experiment 9.20

Clamp the test-tube A and the thermometer B at roughly equal distances (about 10 cm) on either side of the light bulb as shown in Fig. 9.28. Take the readings of both thermometers and write them down.

Now switch on the lamp. Take the temperature on each thermometer at one minute intervals and write them down in two columns as in the table below. Keep on doing this for about 10 minutes.

Time (minutes)	Reading of A	Reading of B
0		
1		
2		
3		

Draw graphs to show each set of results, putting time on the horizontal axis and temperature on the vertical axis. Use crosses for the readings of thermometer A and circles for those of thermometer B.

ig. 9.26 How does white clothing help to keep
ese people cool?

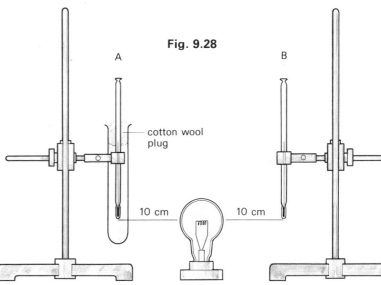

Fig. 9.28

A   B

cotton wool plug

10 cm   10 cm

Which temperature rises faster? Your test-tube is acting like a garden glass-house or greenhouse.

9.9 HOW A GREENHOUSE STAYS WARM

The heat rays from the Sun are very penetrating and easily pass through the glass panes of the greenhouse. Inside the greenhouse these rays heat up the plants and the soil. The heated plants and soil in turn give out heat rays. Since these rays are coming from sources which are much less hot than the Sun, they cannot penetrate back through the glass. When these heat rays get to the glass panes they are reflected back round the inside of the greenhouse.

Very little of the heat which enters the greenhouse by radiation manages to get out again by

Fig. 9.29 A garden greenhouse.

radiation. The greenhouse is therefore a sun-trap. The inside of it gets hotter and hotter. If this were allowed to go on the plants inside might shrivel up. So gardeners sometimes leave some glass panes in the roof open. By what method does the extra heat escape?

Experiment 9.21
Another way of detecting heat radiation

Heat radiation is often called infra red radiation. Try to find out for yourself what this means and why this is a good name for it.

In this experiment you are going to use an **infra red detector**. It contains a special transistor. When infra red energy falls on the transistor it produces an electric current. This can be read on an ammeter. The more energy that falls on the transistor the bigger the current it makes. This special kind of transistor, which is called a **thermistor**, is therefore something like a thermometer.

Put a mark on the base of the thermistor so that you can see where it stands against the scale on the metre rule. Set up the detector a short distance from the heater. Now switch on the heater. You may have to adjust the position of the detector so that the needle on the ammeter does not move off the scale. If it did, this very sensitive instrument would be damaged.

Now note the exact position of the detector mark on the metre scale and take the reading of the meter. Repeat this with the detector at different distances from the heater.

Enter your results in a table. Then draw a graph of your readings, plotting the meter readings (on the vertical axis) against distances from the heater (on the horizontal axis). What can you learn from the graph?

If you double the distance of the detector from the heater does the meter reading fall to a half, as you might expect – or is it nearer to a quarter?

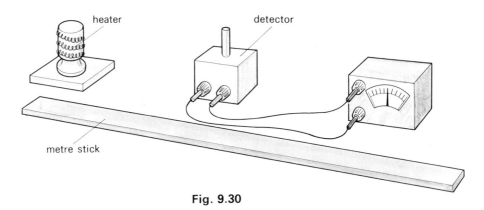

Fig. 9.30

9.10 HEATING OUR HOMES

In this Unit you have learnt how things lose and gain heat. You can usefully summarize your work by considering how our homes are heated.

In the UK the winters are usually quite cold, with snow and ice, and the summers are warm; so we have to keep our homes warm in winter and cool in summer. Many other countries do not have this problem. For instance, in the Caribbean the temperature is very warm all the year round. There the problem is how to keep the house cool. The kind of building is therefore very different from ours.

In this country most of our houses are built of bricks or stone. They have tiled or slated roofs (although there are still some thatched cottages), and they have windows which are made of glass and which can be opened or closed.

Bricks and stone are good insulators. Once the house is warm it tends to stay warm because it does not lose much heat to the outside by conduction. The thickness of the wall helps, too. The thicker the wall the less easily the heat will be lost. Sometimes walls are made of two layers of brick with an air space in between. This is called a 'cavity wall'. It helps to keep in the heat because air is a bad conductor – even worse than solid brick – and because the air is enclosed it cannot move away, so heat cannot be carried away by convection.

The windows, however, are made of glass which is fairly thin. Glass is not a good conductor of heat, but because it is so much thinner than the walls of the house more heat can be lost through the windows than through the walls. Many houses

(a) Stone houses in England.

(b) A Carribean house with louvred windows.

(c) Thatched mud huts in Lesotho.

(d) A white-painted house in Tunisia.

Fig. 9.31 Different types of houses from different countries.

(a) Electric 'fire'. (b) Solid fuel fire. (c) Gas fire.

Fig. 9.32 What are the advantages and disadvantages of each of these ways of heating a room?

now have 'double glazing'. This is just two sheets of glass instead of one, with an air space in between. Why does this keep in the heat better than just one sheet of glass?

Both air and glass are bad conductors. The air between the glass sheets cannot escape, so it cannot carry away heat by convection. Double glazing therefore has the same effect as increasing the thickness of the window, and so it cuts down loss of heat by conduction. Incidentally the noise getting into the room from traffic in the street is also very much less, so double glazing makes rooms quieter as well as warmer.

In the colder weather we have to heat our homes. Many homes now have **central heating**. This is a way of heating the whole house, or perhaps just part of it, from a central supply of heat energy. This central supply may come from burning oil, gas, or solid fuel (such as coke or coal), or from electricity. The heat energy is taken round the house from the central supply usually by hot water, which passes through pipes and radiators. The hot water circulates through the pipes by convection.

The fuel heats up water in a boiler. The hot water rises to the top of the tank. From there it travels round the house through pipes and radiators. On its journey it cools down, and returns to the boiler to be heated up again. The hot water pipes and radiators heat the rooms by causing convection currents, and also to some extent by radiation.

If we do not have a central heating system and want to heat single rooms we use gas fires, electric 'fires', or solid fuel fires. These all make warm air circulate through the room by convection, and also transfer heat energy to the air by radiation.

Night-storage heaters are heated by electricity in 'off-peak' periods – that is, when the demand for electricity is less. To encourage people to use electricity at this time the Electricity Board sells 'off-peak' electricity more cheaply. The storage heater is therefore left switched on all night when people are not using electricity for lighting, and when most factories and offices are not working. The heating element in the heater warms up bricks which keep their heat, only gradually giving it out during the day when the electricity is switched off. At the end of the day the bricks are cool again. They are heated up again the following night, ready for the next day.

In this Unit you have learnt about the way in which heat reaches us from the Sun. Could this radiation be used to heat buildings and warm water? Of course, our homes are heated to some extent by the rays of the Sun, but it is now possible to 'collect' the radiation from the Sun and use it more effectively.

If you look back to page 49 of Book 1 you will see a picture (Fig. 3.33) of a swimming pool which is heated by the heat of the Sun which has been collected with special 'solar panels'. Solar radiation can also be used to provide enough heat to run the hot water system of a house. However, we do not get a great number of really hot sunny days in this country, and it is sometimes necessary to boost the solar heat supply by using electricity, gas, oil, or coal. It is difficult to store solar energy as we receive it from the Sun – though we can do it by using plants. Plants use the Sun's energy to build their bodies. We can then burn the plants – either as wood or as coal – and get the solar energy from them as heat energy. Do you think this is an efficient way of doing it?

Look at the picture of a Caribbean home in Fig. 9.31. Here the problem is how to keep the house cool rather than how to keep it warm; yet at the same time it has to be weather-proof. Sometimes there are very heavy rain-storms and gales, so the people have to have protection against them. Very often the houses in hot countries are made of wood. They do not have windows made of glass, but 'louvres', as you can see in Fig. 9.31. These let the air circulate in and out of the house without letting the rain in. Some homes have large electric fans which make the air move around.

If a house in a hot country has glass windows, then the rooms are often **air-conditioned**. The air-conditioning unit is like the cooling arrangement in a refrigerator, but it also includes a fan which draws the warm air into the 'cooler' and pushes cold air out.

Air-conditioning is also used in this country. The high speed 125 trains have double-glazed windows which cannot be opened. This keeps the noise of the train running over the rails and of the rush of air which is made when the train moves so fast from disturbing the passengers. To keep the temperature of the air comfortable and to maintain ventilation each coach is air-conditioned.

Why do you think each coach has doors which open and close automatically?

The same idea is used in planes. The windows of the plane are double-glazed to keep the noise out. They are also sealed because the cabin is 'pressurized'. So ventilation must be provided by air-conditioning. However, the air-conditioning machine in an aeroplane must pump in air, and then warm it, because when it is flying at great heights, the temperature outside the plane is very low. It may, in fact, be as low as $-35\,°C$.

Something for you to do

Find out how your school and a shop in your town are heated. If you know anyone who works in a factory ask how it is kept warm in winter.

Fig. 9.33 (a) The windows of a 125 train cannot be opened. Why?

9.11 HOUSE INSULATION

To finish your work on heat flow you could do some experiments on the heat insulation of houses. You will need a closed wooden box with a glass plate on one side so that you can see inside.

There should be a bayonet socket and a light bulb inside, and a hole in the top into which a thermometer in a stopper can fit. This box represents a room in a house.

First heat the 'room' to a chosen temperature by switching on the light bulb. Then, after switching off the light, find the time it takes for the temperature to fall by $5\,°C$.

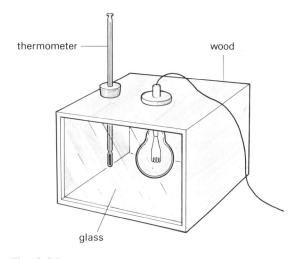

Fig. 9.34

Fig. 9.33 (b) How do these doors help to keep the building warm?

Repeat this experiment with different materials wrapped round the box in turn. They should represent cavity wall insulation, double glazing, the effect of carpeting the floor, the use of loft insulation, etc.

For each type of insulation (that is, for each experiment) note the time it takes for the temperature of the 'room' to fall by 5 °C from the chosen temperature.

WHAT YOU HAVE LEARNT IN THIS UNIT

1 Heat can travel in three ways.
   (a) **Conduction**   Particles in the heated part of the material vibrate more rapidly and make their neighbours vibrate more in turn. In this way the energy is passed on from particle to particle and so heat flows from hot parts to cold parts of a material. Metals are the best conductors, and some metals are better than others. For example, copper is better than iron. Non-metals, liquids, and gases are poor conductors of heat. A bad conductor of heat is called a heat **insulator**. Many heat insulators used in everyday life contain air.
   (b) **Convection**   Heat energy is carried by currents of particles, and so convection can only occur in liquids and gases (fluids). When fluids are heated they expand, and when they are cooled they contract. This makes hot fluids rise, and cool ones fall.
   (c) **Radiation**   Heat energy travels in waves from hot objects to cold objects. These waves do not need a material to carry them, so they can travel in a vacuum. Heat reaches us from the Sun by radiation.
2 Dark surfaces both radiate and absorb heat better than light-coloured or shiny surfaces.

NEW WORDS YOU HAVE MET IN THIS UNIT

conduction
convection   These are all defined in the
insulator   summary above.
radiation

SOME QUESTIONS FOR YOU

1 With what material would you lag a water pipe to stop it freezing in winter? Why?
2 Where would you expect air in a room to be the hotter, near the floor or near the ceiling?
3 Eskimos sometimes live in igloos or snow huts. How can they keep warm in a house made of cold snow?
4 Sometimes sheep are caught in snow drifts. Although they are completely buried they are often found alive after some days. How do they manage to survive?
5 Why are
   (a) teapots often shiny and polished?
   (b) central heating radiators usually painted a dull colour?
   (c) tennis clothes white?
6 Decide which of conduction, convection, or radiation is involved in
   (a) ventilating a room,
   (b) using an infra red lamp,
   (c) using a soldering iron,
   (d) using a tea cosy,
   (e) using a fireman's asbestos suit,
   (f) using a spaceman's suit.
7 Why do birds look 'fat' on a cold day?

UNIT 10

Hydrogen, acids, and alkalis

10.1 ANOTHER GAS

In this Unit you are going to study another gas. You have met it before, but you have not yet found out much about it. It is called **hydrogen**.

You will have a lot of fun with it because it is a gas which makes pops, bangs, and squeals when it burns.

10.2 SOME FACTS ABOUT HYDROGEN

First of all let's find out a few things about hydrogen.

Experiment 10.1
Some properties of hydrogen

Warning   Safety goggles should be worn when you are doing experiments (a) and (b).
(a) Hold a lighted taper close to the mouth of a test-tube of hydrogen. What happens?

Fig. 10.1

(b) Get another tube of hydrogen and push a lighted taper well inside the tube. What happens this time?

Fig. 10.2

(c) Hold a test-tube of hydrogen with its mouth under water in a dish. Does the water rise up into the test-tube? What does this tell you about hydrogen?

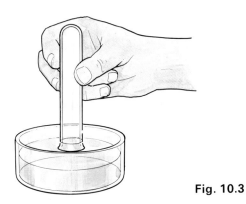

Fig. 10.3

(d) Your teacher will make some bubbles containing hydrogen by passing the gas into soap solution. Do the bubbles rise or fall in the air before they burst?

If you have a cylinder of hydrogen in school your teacher can blow up a balloon with the gas and tie the balloon at the neck. Will the balloon rise or fall when it is released? Try it and see.

As a result of these experiments you have found out the following facts.

1   Hydrogen burns with a very pale blue flame. It is so pale that you can hardly see it. When the lighted taper is put to the mouth of a tube of hydrogen there is a pop. If there is any air mixed with the hydrogen you will hear a peculiar squealing noise. **This is a test for hydrogen.** No other gas burns just like that.
2   Hydrogen does not let a taper burn in it. When you put the lighted taper right inside the tube the gas burned at the mouth of the tube, but the taper went out.
3   Hydrogen does not dissolve in water.
4   Hydrogen is less dense than air. The bubbles of hydrogen and the balloon filled with hydrogen rose in the air.

Compare these properties with those of oxygen. Oxygen does not burn itself, but things burn in it very well indeed. So as far as burning is concerned, hydrogen seems to be the opposite of oxygen.

You will remember that oxygen dissolves a little in water – if it did not do this fish could not live. Hydrogen does not seem to dissolve at all.

Oxygen is very slightly more dense than air, whereas hydrogen is much less dense than air. In fact hydrogen is the lightest gas known.

A question for you

If you wanted to collect a jar of hydrogen from a cylinder which way up would you hold the jar – as in Fig. 10.4(a) or Fig. 10.4(b)?

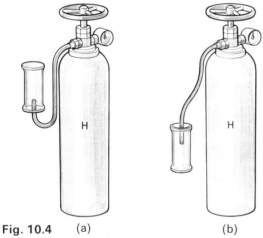

Fig. 10.4   (a)   (b)

You found out that hydrogen burns with a pop. This pop was a slight explosion which happened because the hydrogen gas had a little air mixed with it. A mixture of hydrogen and oxygen explodes very loudly when a lighted taper is brought near it. The explosion is particularly loud when there is twice as much hydrogen as oxygen in the mixture.

10.3 WHAT IS FORMED WHEN HYDROGEN IS BURNED?

Experiment 10.2

You should wear safety goggles when doing this experiment.
Fill a *dry* test-tube with *dry* hydrogen from a cylinder. Burn it as you did in Experiment 10.1(a).

Look at the sides of the tube. Can you see anything there?

Sprinkle a little anhydrous copper(II) sulphate into the tube. What happens to the copper(II) sulphate?

Burn another tube of dry hydrogen and this time put a piece of blue cobalt chloride paper inside the tube. What happens to it?

You learned in Unit 8 that water turns anhydrous copper(II) sulphate from white to blue, and it also turns blue cobalt chloride pink. So you have discovered that the tiny drops which you saw on the side of the tube in which you burned hydrogen contained water.

Notice that we cannot say that the liquid *is* water as a result of these tests alone. Milk, lemonade, Coke, and many other liquids will turn anhydrous copper(II) sulphate blue – just because they *contain* water. How could you be certain that the liquid formed when hydrogen burns *is* water and nothing else? You would have to find its freezing point and its boiling point. Water is the only liquid which freezes at 0 °C and boils at 100 °C.

Of course, to do this you would need much more of the liquid than you got by burning a test-tube full of hydrogen. You would have to burn dry hydrogen at a jet and collect the liquid formed, so that you had a few cubic centimetres of the liquid to test.

This can be done by using the apparatus shown in Fig. 10.5.

Fig. 10.5

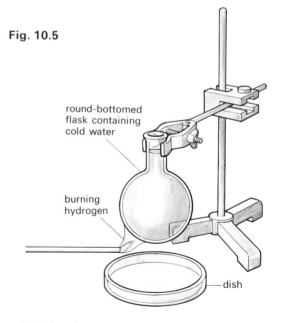

round-bottomed flask containing cold water

burning hydrogen

dish

This is a dangerous experiment because, as you have learnt, hydrogen mixed with air explodes when a flame is put to it. If any air becomes mixed with the hydrogen while the experiment is taking place the whole apparatus will blow up. It is best, therefore, not to attempt it. Your teacher may, however, be able to show you a film of the experiment being carried out.

These experiments show that hydrogen combines with oxygen to form water. The reaction is very vigorous. Hydrogen burns with a very hot flame; and a mixture of hydrogen and oxygen explodes violently. So a great deal of energy, which was in the hydrogen and the oxygen, is changed into other forms (mainly heat) when these two gases combine.

10.4 BREAKING UP WATER

If water is made from hydrogen and oxygen it should be possible to break water down again into these gases. You have seen that a lot of energy is changed into heat when hydrogen and oxygen combine. To get the gases back from water we would expect to have to put all this energy back again – and this is no easy job!

Can this be done just by heating the water? Well, you know what happens when you do that. The water simply boils! What about heating steam, then? (Steam is only water in the form of gas.) Scientists have found that it *is* possible to break up steam into hydrogen and oxygen by heating it very strongly indeed – but the temperatures required are so high that the experiment cannot be carried out successfully in a school laboratory.

There is, however, another way of breaking down compounds. Do you remember how you broke down copper(II) chloride into copper and chlorine in Unit 4? Let's try the same idea with water. We shall try to break down water by passing an electric current through it.

Experiment 10.3
Breaking down water

Safety goggles should be worn when testing the gases in this experiment.

Set up a circuit like the one shown in Fig. 10.6.

When you put pure water in the apparatus is there any reading on the meter? Clearly water does not conduct electricity very well – in fact, pure water is almost non-conducting, it is almost an insulator.

Now add some sodium fluoride to the water. Sodium fluoride is a compound of sodium and fluorine only; it does not contain any hydrogen or oxygen. Does the

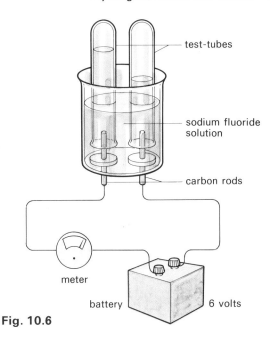

test-tubes

sodium fluoride solution

carbon rods

meter

battery   6 volts

Fig. 10.6

meter show a reading now? Collect the gases given off in the two test-tubes. Find out whether they burn, or if they let things burn better in them than in air. Is the volume of gas in the two tubes the same?

You were able to break up water into hydrogen and oxygen in this experiment – but only after you had added some sodium fluoride to the water. It is possible to use other substances in place of the sodium fluoride; and, in fact, the sodium fluoride is not used up at all.

A question for you

How could you prove that the sodium fluoride is not used up in this experiment?

You will have noticed that the volume of the hydrogen formed when you broke down water in this experiment was just about twice the volume of the oxygen formed. So you can conclude that when hydrogen combines with oxygen to form water, two volumes of hydrogen combine with one volume of oxygen. This means that 100 cm³ of hydrogen would combine with 50 cm³ of oxygen; 10 cm³ of hydrogen would combine with 5 cm³ of oxygen, and so on.

A question for you

What volume of oxygen would combine with 1 litre of hydrogen? What volume of hydrogen would combine with 1 litre of oxygen to form water?

10.5 SOME ODD METALS

Some time ago you came across the metal calcium (Unit I) and tried putting a piece of it into water. Repeat this experiment now just to remind yourself what happens.

Experiment 10.4
Calcium and water

You should wear safety goggles when doing this experiment.

Calcium corrodes very easily. When this happens a layer of calcium oxide forms on its surface. Before starting the experiment scrape a few small pieces of calcium with a knife to remove this layer. You will then see the shiny surface of the metal.

Put two or three small pieces of calcium into about 5 cm of water in a test-tube. What happens? Hold your thumb over the end of the tube for a few seconds so that the gas cannot escape. Then hold a lighted taper near the end of the tube as you take your thumb away. What happens? What gas is given off?

Look at the liquid in the tube. It is now milky. Put a piece of indicator paper into the liquid. What happens to it? This tells you that the liquid is no longer water, but an alkali.

Filter some of the liquid. Collect a little of the filtrate in a test-tube, and blow into it through a tube. What happens?

The exhaled air you blew through the liquid contained more carbon dioxide than the air around us. You found that the liquid turned cloudy. In Unit 8 you met a solution which turns cloudy when carbon dioxide is passed through it. The solution was calcium hydroxide (or lime water).

So, when calcium reacts with water, hydrogen and calcium hydroxide are formed. This can be written as a word equation as follows:

calcium + water → calcium hydroxide + hydrogen

There are some other metals which behave in the same sort of way as calcium when they are added to water. One of these is **sodium**. Sodium reacts so easily with oxygen in the air that it is kept under oil to stop the air getting to it. Sodium metal is so soft that it can be cut with a knife.

Experiment 10.5
Sodium and water

This is a dangerous experiment which will be done by your teacher. You should keep well away from the bench.

Your teacher will cut a small piece of sodium and put it onto some water in a trough. What happens? Unfortunately it is too dangerous to try to collect the gas given off in this reaction.

After the experiment is complete you can test the liquid in the trough with indicator paper. You will find that, like the liquid left in the calcium experiment (10.4), it is alkaline. It contains sodium hydroxide.

When sodium acts on water, hydrogen is given off and sodium hydroxide is formed. This can be stated in a word equation as follows:

sodium + water → sodium hydroxide + hydrogen

You will have noticed that the reaction of sodium and water was much more vigorous than when calcium acted on water.

Experiment 10.6
Magnesium and water

Put some magnesium powder wrapped up in a small piece of tissue paper in a test-tube containing water as shown in Fig. 10.7.

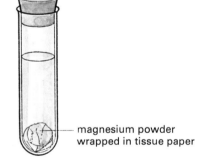

magnesium powder wrapped in tissue paper

Fig. 10.7

You may have to wait for several days before you see any change. Test the gas which collects to see if it is hydrogen. What do you find?

Magnesium and water react together very slowly. Hydrogen is given off. Can you think of any ways of making the reaction faster?

You will remember that for reaction to take place molecules of the reacting substances must hit each other. You know that when molecules are heated they move faster, and so there will be more hits per second. So perhaps one way of making the reaction quicker is to use steam instead of water.

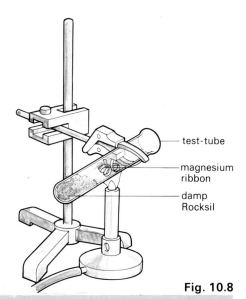

- test-tube
- magnesium ribbon
- damp Rocksil

Fig. 10.8

Experiment 10.7
Magnesium and steam

This is another rather dangerous experiment which will therefore be shown to you by your teacher. You should wear safety goggles while watching it.

The apparatus is shown in Fig. 10.8.

There is some damp Rocksil at the bottom of the test-tube. Further up the tube is a coil of magnesium ribbon. (Magnesium ribbon must be used in this experiment, not magnesium powder. Why do you think this is so?) Heat the magnesium ribbon. The heat is generally enough to boil the water in the damp Rocksil, and this steam passes over the hot magnesium. If the water does not boil it can be warmed by moving the burner down towards the Rocksil.

You will see a gas burning at the end of the test-tube. This cannot be steam because steam does not burn. It is hydrogen. The reaction is often so strong that the tube melts with the heat.

You have seen that while magnesium reacts very slowly with cold water, it reacts vigorously with steam.

You have now tried the action of three metals on water. You have found that the strength of the reaction is different with each metal. Would you agree that of them all sodium had the greatest reaction with **cold** water, calcium next, and magnesium third?

Experiment 10.8
Other metals and steam

The apparatus used in Experiment 10.7 can be used to find out about the action of other metals on steam. Try the experiment with zinc, iron, tin, lead, and copper.

You will find that these metals react more slowly than magnesium does, and some do not react at all.

You could arrange the metals in order of their reactivity with water. The order of activity would be

sodium	reacts strongly with cold water
calcium	reacts less strongly with cold water
magnesium	reacts very slowly with cold water but strongly with steam
zinc	reacts less strongly with steam
iron	reacts very little with steam
tin, lead, copper	no result

10.6 ACIDS

Acids have often been mentioned in this book. The word 'acid' means 'sour'. We often say that a sour liquid tastes 'acid'. Think of some sour things you come across at home. What about vinegar, lemon juice, grapefruit juice, tartaric acid, citric acid, and sour milk? All these are acids, or mixtures of acids. Vinegar contains acetic acid, lemon juice and grapefruit juice contain citric acid (lemons, grapefruit, and oranges are called 'citrus' fruits), and sour milk contains lactic acid.

10.7 METALS AND ACIDS

All acids contain hydrogen, so perhaps you can obtain hydrogen from them. You will remember that you got hydrogen from water by adding certain metals to it. Perhaps you can do the same with acids. Let us find out.

Two common acids found in the laboratory are hydrochloric acid and sulphuric acid. We generally use them in the diluted form – that is, mixed with water. Many acids, particularly when concentrated (the scientist's word for undiluted) are very dangerous and have to be handled very carefully. They are much less dangerous when diluted but they can still burn holes in your clothes – so be careful!

Experiment 10.9
Metals and acids

Wear safety goggles when doing this experiment.

In this experiment half the class will use hydrochloric acid and half will use sulphuric acid. Your teacher will tell you which you will need.

Put about 5 cm depth of dilute acid in 5 different test-tubes in a stand. Add a piece of magnesium ribbon to one tube. What happens? Test the gas given off for hydrogen. Does the tube get warm? Was the reaction very fast?

In the second tube try the experiment again, but this time use a piece of zinc foil instead of the magnesium.

In the other tubes try copper foil, aluminium foil, and iron filings.

Note down your results in a table like the one below.

Acid		
Strong reaction	*Weak reaction*	*No. reaction*

List the metals in order of activity. Is it the same as the order you found for the activity of metals with water?

10.8 WHAT HAPPENS TO THE METAL?

You will probably be asking 'Where has the metal gone when it reacts with the acid?' Let us think about the reaction between magnesium and dilute hydrochloric acid. Hydrogen was given off; but there is clearly no magnesium in hydrogen. Hydrogen is an element; it contains nothing but hydrogen.

Is the solution of magnesium in dilute acid like the solution of salt in water? If it is you ought to be able to get the magnesium back by evaporating the solution. Let's see if this is possible.

Experiment 10.10
What happens to the metal when it reacts with an acid?

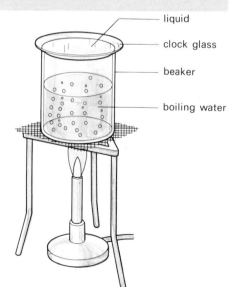

Fig. 10.9

Pour some of the solution left after magnesium has been acted upon by dilute hydrochloric acid into a glass dish. Put this on top of a beaker containing water (Fig. 10.9)

Boil the water. The steam from the boiling water heats the liquid in the glass dish, and makes the water evaporate from it. Is anything left in the dish? Is it magnesium?

You have found that a white substance is left on the glass dish. It certainly does not look like magnesium; it looks more like salt. Yet the magnesium must still be there somewhere.

The only place where it can be is in the white stuff. This substance is magnesium chloride. It contains magnesium combined with chlorine.

You will understand how it has been formed if you remember that hydrochloric acid is a solution of hydrogen chloride in water. The magnesium has pushed out the hydrogen from the hydrogen chloride, and has combined with the chloride part. A word equation for this reaction can be written like this:

magnesium + hydrogen chloride
    →magnesium chloride + hydrogen

From your experiments you have found that some metals push out hydrogen more easily than others. Magnesium, zinc, and iron do this quite easily, whereas copper will not do it at all. Clearly the magnesium, the zinc, and the iron have a greater 'pull' on chlorine than hydrogen has, whereas copper has a weaker 'pull'.

The compound magnesium chloride is called a **salt**. There are many thousands of different salts since most metals will react with a large number of acids. The most common salt of all is sodium chloride, which is often, therefore, called common salt. It is the salt we put on our food, and which we use in cooking. It is found in large quantities in the sea and, in some parts of the world, on land.

A question for you

Dilute sulphuric acid is the common name for a solution of hydrogen sulphate in water. What salt would be formed when magnesium reacts with dilute sulphuric acid?

Magnesium sulphate is sold in shops as Epsom salts. Find out how it got this name, and what it is used for.

10.9 TESTING FOR ACIDS

Although we have said that acids taste sour, it is not very wise to use the sense of taste to find out whether a substance is an acid. Some acids are very strong and can burn you badly. Some are poisonous. Remember that **you should never taste anything in the laboratory unless you know that it is harmless**. Your teacher knows what is harmless and what is dangerous. So do not taste anything unless you are told to do so.

Instead of tasting to find out whether a substance is an acid, we use the fact that acids change the colour of some dyes. One of these is litmus. It is not, in fact, used very much as a dye because it washes out of fabrics very easily, and because it changes colour when it comes into contact with acids and alkalis. It is obtained from a small plant which grows chiefly in South America, but nowadays it can be made artificially.

Filter paper dipped into a solution of litmus and allowed to dry is called litmus paper. Because the dye can be used to test (or indicate) whether or not a liquid is acid, it is called an **indicator**.

Experiment 10.11
Testing for acids

Obtain small amounts of different acids. If the acid is solid dissolve a little of it in water in a test-tube. Dip a piece of indicator paper into each liquid. What happens to the paper?

Now try dipping a piece of indicator paper into water and into a solution of salt. Can the paper be used to find out whether a liquid is acidic?

We use a scale to measure acidity. It is called the **pH scale** and runs from 0 to 14. If a solution is acidic its pH is less than 7.

The alkalis form another class of substances. In some respects, as you will see, they are the opposite of acids. Alkalis have a pH greater than 7. A solution of an alkali is said to be alkaline.

A liquid which has a pH of exactly 7 is said to be **neutral**. It is neither acidic nor alkaline.

The pH scale does not measure how concentrated an acid is. It shows how good an acid the liquid is. You can have very concentrated solutions of acids which are yet not strong acids. Thus vinegar can be very concentrated (that is, it may have quite a large mass of acid dissolved in say, a litre of water) yet, compared to quite

dilute hydrochloric acid, it is very sluggish when it acts on a metal. Although it is more concentrated than the hydrochloric acid it is a weaker acid.

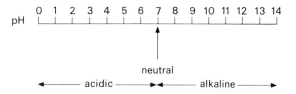

Fig. 10.10

Experiment 10.12
Testing for alkalis

Here is a list of substances you will find in the laboratory: solutions of sodium hydroxide, sodium carbonate, calcium hydroxide, sodium hydrogencarbonate, ammonia. Dip a piece of indicator paper into a little of each of them, using a fresh piece of paper each time. What happens to the colour of the paper?

Some kinds of indicator paper change to different colours according to the pH of the liquid they are placed in. These are called 'universal indicators'. They change colour over a wide range of tints because a mixture of dyes is used. You will find a colour chart on a packet of universal indicator paper (or pH paper, as it is sometimes called) which shows what colour the paper turns for different pH values.

Experiment 10.13

Test some of the following liquids with pH paper: soda water (a solution of carbon dioxide in water), lemonade, orange juice, milk, Coca-cola, etc.

Put your results in a table like the one below.

Liquid	pH	Acid, alkaline, or neutral

What can you say about the liquids you usually like to drink?

We have said that in some ways alkalis are the opposite of acids. What do you think will happen if you mix an acid solution with an alkaline one?

If they are opposites perhaps they will cancel each other out, and destroy each other. The next experiment will help you find out what does happen.

Experiment 10.14
What happens when an acid is mixed with an alkali?

You will need a dilute solution of sodium hydroxide and some dilute hydrochloric acid. Test the pH of each with pH paper.

The sodium hydroxide is an alkali (pH greater than 7), and the hydrochloric acid is, of course, an acid (pH less than 7).

Measure 10 cm³ of the sodium hydroxide solution into a dish, using a graduated syringe. Add 2 drops of universal indicator solution.

Fill a graduated syringe with the acid solution and add it, 0.5 cm³ at a time, to the alkali solution. Stir the liquid after each addition, and notice the colour of the indicator. Note also the pH of the liquid from the colour chart.

Put down your results in a table like this:

Volume of acid added (cm³)	Colour	pH
0 0.5 1 1.5		

Did the acid 'cancel out' the alkali? We call this 'cancelling out' **neutralization**. The acid **neutralized** the alkali; and, of course, the alkali neutralized the acid.

As you know, the liquid is neutral when the pH is 7. How much acid did you have to add to neutralize the alkali?

What happened to the pH if you added more acid than this?

10.10 WHAT IS PRODUCED WHEN AN ACID NEUTRALIZES AN ALKALI?

As both the acid and the alkali neutralize each other, both are destroyed and something new must be formed. Let us find out what it is.

Experiment 10.15

Measure 10 cm³ of the same sodium hydroxide solution you used in the last experiment into a dish. Add to it

the volume of hydrochloric acid that you found just neutralized it, but this time do not put in any indicator. Stir the liquid with a glass rod. To make sure that the liquid really is neutral take out a drop of it on a glass rod and touch it on to indicator paper. If it is not quite right add a drop or two of acid or alkali, whichever is required. Then evaporate the solution as you did in Experiment 10.10. What is left at the bottom of the dish?

A new substance has been produced. It is the compound sodium chloride. When an acid neutralizes an alkali a salt is formed. Of course, it is not always sodium chloride. You got sodium chloride because you started with sodium hydroxide and hydrochloric acid.

This chemical reaction can be put into a word equation.

sodium hydroxide + hydrogen chloride
(hydrochloric acid)
→sodium chloride + hydrogen hydroxide
(water)

You already know that hydrochloric acid is a solution of hydrogen chloride in water – that is why we have written hydrogen chloride above hydrochloric acid in the above equation. Similarly, water can be called hydrogen hydroxide. By writing the equation in this form we see that in neutralization there is a 'change of partners'. You have met this kind of reaction before.

If you had used the alkali potassium hydroxide with sulphuric acid (which, you will remember, is hydrogen sulphate), you would have got potassium sulphate. The word equation for this reaction is

potassium hydroxide + hydrogen sulphate
(sulphuric acid)
→ potassium sulphate + hydrogen hydroxide
(water)

How do you think you would make sodium sulphate, calcium chloride, and potassium nitrate? Work out what acids and alkalis you would use.

In Experiment 10.14 you found that every member of the class got the same result for the volume of acid required to neutralize a certain volume of sodium hydroxide solution. This, of course, was because you were all using the same solutions. What would have happened if some members of the class were using solutions of different concentrations?

Suppose your group was using 10 cm³ of a solution which contained 0.5 g of sodium hydroxide, while your neighbours used 10 cm³ of a solution which contained only 0.25 g of sodium hydroxide. Suppose, too, that both groups neutralized their solutions with hydrochloric acid of the same concentration. Would the second group require more, less, or the same volume of acid to neutralize their solution?

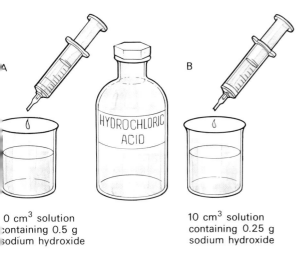

0 cm³ solution containing 0.5 g sodium hydroxide

10 cm³ solution containing 0.25 g sodium hydroxide

Fig. 10.11

If A (Fig. 10.11) required 20 cm³ of acid to neutralize it, how much would B require?

1   10 cm³
2   20 cm³
3   40 cm³

Now see whether you have got the right answer by trying an experiment.

Experiment 10.16

You will be given a solution which contains 1 g of sodium hydroxide in 20 cm³ of solution. Measure out 10 cm³ of this solution with a syringe. What mass of sodium hydroxide does it contain? Find out how many cm³ of hydrochloric acid are needed to neutralize it.

Now take 10 cm³ of the solution of sodium hydroxide, measuring it out with a syringe as before. Add 10 cm³ of water to it and stir. What mass of sodium hydroxide is there in the 20 cm³ of solution?

Measure out 10 cm³ of this solution with a syringe. How much sodium hydroxide is there in the 10 cm³? Find out what volume of hydrochloric acid is needed to neutralize it.

Compare the masses of sodium hydroxide taken in these two experiments with the volumes of acid required to neutralize them. Can you see any connection?

Is it the volume of solution that is important, or the mass of sodium hydroxide there? In the last experiment you took the same volume of sodium hydroxide solution (10 cm³ each time) but the solutions were of different strengths. To answer our question we must take solutions of sodium hydroxide which contain the same mass of solute in different volumes of solution.

Experiment 10.17

Using a syringe, measure 10 cm³ of the sodium hydroxide solution into each of three beakers, A, B, and C. To beaker B add 20 cm³ of water and to beaker C add 40 cm³ of water. Now find out what volume of hydrochloric acid is needed to neutralize the alkali in each beaker.

Did you expect this result? You had three solutions with different volumes, yet they were all neutralized by the same volume of acid. Now think about the mass of sodium hydroxide in each beaker. It was the same each time, wasn't it? All you did was to add more and more water to the beakers. You did not alter the mass of alkali present.

The neutralization of an acid by an alkali is, of course, a chemical reaction. Two substances were mixed together and new substances were formed. This is the first time you have actually thought about the masses of substances that react together. You found that a given mass of sodium hydroxide always reacts with a definite, unchanging mass of hydrochloric acid. The same is true of any chemical reaction; substances always react together in one fixed ratio of mass. Thus, 24 g of magnesium *always* combine with 16 g of oxygen to form magnesium oxide; 1 g of hydrogen *always* combines with 8 g of oxygen to form water; 56 g of iron *always* combine with 32 g of sulphur to form iron(II) sulphide; 63.5 g of copper *always* combine with 71 g of chlorine to form copper(II) chloride.

This is a very important chemical law. It is called the **law of constant composition**.

10.11 NEUTRALIZATION PUT TO USE

We can use the fact that acids and alkalis neutralize each other in our everyday life.

You may at some time have been stung by an insect, such as a bee or a wasp, or by a plant like a nettle. When a bee stings you it injects acid into you. To neutralize the sting you could rub on an alkali. Of course, it must not be a very strong alkali like sodium hydroxide, or the effect on your skin would be very harmful. It would have to be a very mild alkali, such as sodium hydrogencarbonate (baking soda). When a bee stings you it actually leaves part of its body, called the 'sting', in your flesh. Before treating the swollen area with alkali the sting must be pulled out.

A wasp does not leave its sting in your flesh. It injects an alkali into you. To neutralize it you would add an acid – not a strong acid like hydrochloric or sulphuric acid, but a weak one, such as vinegar.

Indigestion is often caused by too much acid in the stomach. You may have seen some indigestion tablets labelled 'antacids'. This just means that they get rid of acid – they are 'anti-acids'. Can you guess what kind of a substance an anti-acid is? It is, of course, an alkali. That is why substances like sodium hydrogencarbonate (baking soda), magnesium hydroxide (magnesia) and magnesium carbonate, which are all weak alkalis, are used to ease indigestion.

Some plants will not grow well in soil which is too acid. Farmers often have to reduce the amount of acid in the soil to improve their crops.

Experiment 10.18
Testing soil for acidity

Bring about a tablespoon of soil from your garden to school. Put it in a jam-jar or beaker and cover it with water. Stir it well and then dip an indicator paper into the liquid. From the colour chart for the indicator you will be able to say what the pH of the soil is.

If the soil is too acid the farmer adds lime to 'cure' or 'sweeten' it. An acid soil is sometimes said to be 'sour' (you know why) so you can see where the idea of 'sweetening' it comes from. Lime, or calcium hydroxide (its proper chemical name), is a very mild alkali. Because it is not very soluble in water (you will remember that a solution of it is called lime water) it does not get washed out of the soil as soon as it rains.

Fig. 10.12 Too much rich food!

WHAT YOU HAVE LEARNT IN THIS UNIT

1   Hydrogen is a gas which burns in air with a pop. It does not dissolve in water. It is the lightest gas known.

2   Water is formed when hydrogen burns in air. This suggests that water is a compound of hydrogen and oxygen – an oxide of hydrogen. Two volumes of hydrogen combine with one volume of oxygen.

3   Some metals, such as calcium and sodium, break up cold water: one of the products is hydrogen. Other metals, such as magnesium, zinc, and iron, can break up steam. Copper and silver cannot do this.

4   The metals can be put in an order of activity according to the ease with which they break up water. The order is

sodium, calcium, magnesium, aluminium,
          zinc, iron, tin, lead, copper, silver
          most reactive ⟶ least reactive

5 Hydrogen can also be obtained from dilute acids by adding certain metals. For example, zinc and magnesium give hydrogen when they are added to dilute hydrochloric acid.

6 The order of activity of metals with acids is the same as that with water.

7 When a metal reacts with an acid a salt is formed.

8 Acids neutralize alkalis. When an acid neutralizes an alkali a salt and water are formed.

9 The process of neutralization is of importance in everyday life, for example in relieving the effects of stings, in indigestion remedies, and in correcting the acidity of the soil.

10 The mass of hydrochloric acid which neutralizes a certain mass of sodium hydroxide is always the same. This is an example of the law of constant composition.

NEW WORDS YOU HAVE MET IN THIS UNIT

acid a substance with a sour taste which turns the indicator litmus red, and reacts with an alkali to form a salt and water only.

activity series the metals placed in order of the vigour of their reaction with water or acids.

alkali a substance which turns red litmus blue and reacts with an acid to form a salt and water only.

indicator a dye, or mixture of dyes, which changes colour when an acid or an alkali is added to it.

neutralization the action of an acid on an alkali whereby the properties of both are completely changed and a salt is formed.

neutral a substance is neutral when it has no effect on an indicator such as litmus.

pH the scale of acidity. Acids have a pH less than 7; alkalis have a pH greater than 7. A neutral solution has pH 7.

salt the product of the action of an acid on an alkali. Salts are usually solid at ordinary temperatures.

universal indicator a mixture of dyes which has different colours at different pH values. It can therefore be used to find the pH of a solution.

SOME QUESTIONS FOR YOU

1 Make a list of as many differences as you can between hydrogen and oxygen.

2 When gas A is burnt in air the products are water and a gas which turns lime water milky. What elements *must* the gas contain? Could it contain others? Give reasons for your answers.

3 A liquid has a pH of 3. Is it acidic or alkaline? If a piece of red litmus paper were dipped into the liquid what would happen to the colour of the litmus? If a piece of magnesium ribbon were added to the liquid, what do you think would happen?

4 Name the salts that would be produced when
   (a) calcium hydroxide is neutralized by hydrochloric acid;
   (b) magnesium hydroxide is neutralized by nitric acid;
   (c) sodium hydroxide is neutralized by acetic acid;
   (d) iron(III) hydroxide is neutralized by sulphuric acid.

5 10 cm^3 of hydrochloric acid containing 18.0 g of the acid per litre are neutralized by 15 cm^3 of a certain solution of sodium hydroxide.
   (a) What volume of the acid would be neutralized by 45 cm^3 of the sodium hydroxide?
   (b) What volume of the sodium hydroxide would be required to neutralize 10 cm^3 of a solution of hydrochloric acid containing 36 g of the acid per litre?

6 A copper vessel has become very blackened. The black coating is copper(II) oxide. Which of the following would you use to polish it without dissolving away the metal itself: washing soda, lemon juice, nitric acid, water?

UNIT 11

Detecting the environment

11.1 HOW DO WE FIND OUT?

In earlier Units you found out about yourself and your surroundings. You will remember from Unit I that all our information comes to us through our senses. Very early on you found that sometimes your senses could mislead you. This point will be looked at again later in this Unit. You are now going to find out some fascinating things about your senses. Start by investigating the sense you are using while reading this book. Which one is that?

11.2 THE EYE AND LIGHT

Can you imagine what life must be like for those boys and girls who cannot see? We too often take seeing for granted and do not take care of our eyes. Our eyes are the most sensitive instrument that the body has to find out about its **environment** so we should take care of them. You already know that in some science experiments you must wear goggles to protect your eyes. Some people wear protective dark glasses to cut down the bright light from the Sun.

To find out more about your own eyes you will either watch your teacher cut up a bullock's eye, or you may do this for yourself.

Experiment 11.1
Dissecting a bullock's eye

Before you cut open the eye have a close look at it and try to recognize all the parts labelled in Fig. 11.1. Touch the eye and notice that it feels rubbery, just as if it were made from tough plastic. In fact the white outside layer of the eye (called the **sclerotic coat**) is very tough. Why?

To find out about the inside of the eye you must cut through this coat. The tools must be very sharp and have to be handled carefully.

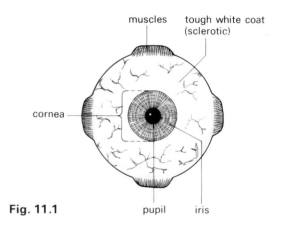

Fig. 11.1

Hold the bullock's eye above a glass dish. Start by making a small cut with a razor blade or a very sharp scalpel just behind the **iris** and the clear **cornea**. Cut round in a circle keeping about the same distance from the iris. You can use scissors to do this. This circular cut will remove the clear cornea and a watery liquid (called the **aqueous humour**) will run out into the dish.

You will probably find that the iris is removed with the cornea, and the black rear surface should be visible, with muscles lying just like the spokes of a wheel. The coloured iris can be removed from the cornea by scraping round the edge with the scalpel. If it is washed in water, it can be turned over to show the coloured front side.

You can see that the black spot in the middle of the iris is simply a hole through which light gets into the eye. Look at the diagram below to find out what this hole is called.

Fig. 11.2

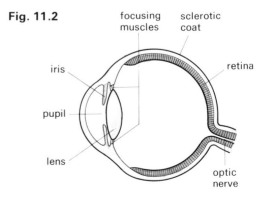

Now look at the eyeball again. Behind the iris you can see a little ball of jelly resting in a bed of softer jelly called **vitreous humour**. (The names 'aqueous humour' and 'vitreous humour' are very old, and go back to the time when doctors first found out what the eye was like.)

This little ball of jelly is called the **lens**. Pick it out with a pair of forceps, and wash out the vitreous humour from the eyeball. You will then see the inside layer of the eyeball, called the **retina**. The retina is lined with very sensitive nerve endings.

Hold up the lens on a pin and try placing it just above a sheet of paper. Do you see anything appearing on the paper when the classroom lights are switched on?

Look through the lens at some printing. What effect does the lens have?

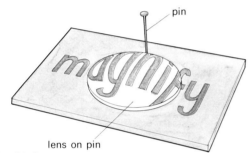
pin

lens on pin

Fig. 11.3

Did you see that the lens acted rather like a 'burning glass' and brought rays of light together on to the paper? It also acted rather like a magnifying glass on the printing. Squeeze the lens gently. Can you change its shape? Does the squeezing have any effect on the size of the printing you see through the lens?

You found that the dark **pupil** in the eye is actually an opening which lets light into the eye. This light goes through the lens and lands on the retina.

Ask your partner to cover his or her eyes for one minute. As soon as they are uncovered, look carefully into them. What do the pupils look like? You should have noticed that while the eyes were covered the pupils grew larger.

Now ask your partner to look out of the window at a bright patch of light. What happens to the size of the pupils now?

It is the iris which changes the size of the pupils. In the dark the iris opens the pupil wider to let more light in. In bright light the iris closes up the pupil to let only a little light into the eye. This protects the retina.

At the end of this experiment your hands and any instruments you have used while cutting and examining the eye must be washed thoroughly.

Experiment 11.2
The blind spot

Fig. 11.4

Cover up your left eye with your left hand and then look hard at the + above. Now move your head slowly towards the page. What do you notice?

When your eye is about 15 cm away from the page something strange happens. The dot disappears. So we are actually blind at that place. You have found what is called your blind spot. Your left eye has a similar blind spot. This means that when you look to the front there are two places, one to the right and the other to the left, where you would not see something that was coming towards you from the front. This is often important.

What does a boxer do so that he is not hit by a punch from his 'blind side'?

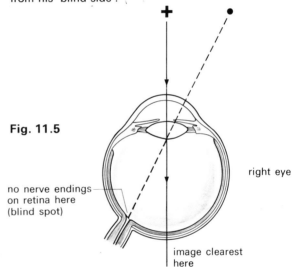

Fig. 11.5

right eye

no nerve endings on retina here (blind spot)

image clearest here

There is nothing wrong with your eye which makes it blind. This spot in your eye is blind because there is no retina at one point. It is where the **optic nerve** enters the retina.

11.3 A KING'S REVENGE

It is said that when King Charles I was in prison in the Tower of London waiting to be executed, he invited the executioner to visit him. He sat at one end of the cell. The King sat about 5 metres away from him, and, covering his left eye, looked about 1.5 metres to the executioner's right. What do you think happened? Try it yourself by getting your partner to act the executioner by sitting very still about 5 metres away. Do you seem to chop off your partner's head?

11.4 THE CAMERA AND THE LENS

Nowadays scientists are able to make instruments which do marvellous things, but as yet no-one has been able to make anything which works as well as your eyes. You are now going to do an experiment which will help you to understand how the lens works.

> ### Experiment 11.3
> *Making a pin-hole camera*

Set up the apparatus shown in Fig. 11.6.

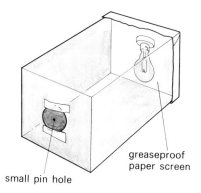

greaseproof paper screen

small pin hole

Fig. 11.6

A chalk box or a small shoe box is about the right size. Cut a square hole in one end and cover it with greaseproof paper. In the opposite end cut a round hole about the size of a ten-pence piece. Stick a piece of thick black paper over this with a piece of sticky tape. Make a small pin-hole in the black paper and face it towards a lighted torch bulb.

It is a good idea to dim the overhead lights at this stage so that you can see more clearly. What can you see on the greaseproof paper screen? Is it the right way up?

The apparatus you have made is called a pin-hole camera. Perhaps you will have time to put a special kind of photographic paper at the back of the box instead of the greaseproof paper. You could then make a photograph of the bulb.

Move the bulb towards the camera. What happens to the size of the picture?

Lay the bulb on its side. What happens to the picture?

You should have found that the picture in the pin-hole camera is upside down and the wrong way round. As you moved the bulb towards the camera the picture got bigger. What do you think happens to the size of the picture when you move the bulb further away?

The picture on your screen is probably rather faint because not much light will be getting through the small pin-hole you made. Can you suggest how you could get more light through to the screen?

Some of you might try making the hole bigger. Others might try making several more holes close to the first one. Are either of these ideas any good?

Although making the hole larger makes the image brighter, it makes it blurred. Making more holes simply makes more separate pictures, all overlapping each other.

11.5 ACTION OF THE LENS

> ### Experiment 11.4
> *Using a convex lens*

Push a pencil right through the black paper of your camera to make one big hole about 1 cm across. Slide a **convex lens** over this hole and move the lens gradually further away from the hole. (A convex lens is one that is thicker in the middle than at the edges.) You should find that at a certain distance you get a bright, sharp, **inverted** (upside down) picture of the bulb **focused** on the screen. This picture is called the **image** of the bulb.

The lens in a camera is moved in the same way to give a clear picture. You will be looking at the camera in greater detail later on. You have just discovered that the lens allows a wide hole (or **aperture**) to be used to let a lot of light into the box. At the same time, if it is in the right position, the lens makes the image sharp.

Let us stop for a moment to compare the eye and the camera. Can you say what the following parts of the eye do?

The iris, the pupil, the lens, the retina, the nerve to the brain.

Look back a few pages if you have forgotten.

Which of these parts of the eye work like each of the following parts of the camera?

The aperture, the lens, the screen.

11.6 SOME FOCUSING EXPERIMENTS

Experiment 11.5
Using thin and thick convex lenses

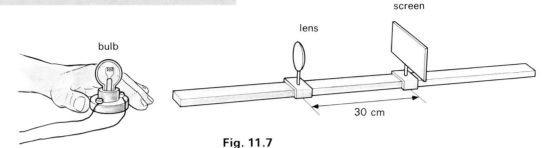

Fig. 11.7

It is best to have the room dimmed for this experiment. Set up the apparatus shown in the diagram. Switch on the bulb and move it slowly backwards and forwards until you get a sharp picture on the screen. Now measure the distance between the bulb and this lens and make a note of it.

Replace the lens with a thicker one. Do not move the lens or the screen. Again move the bulb until you get a sharp picture. Measure the distance from the bulb to this lens.

You should have found that when you used a thin lens, the bulb had to be much further away to give a sharp image than when you used a thick lens. We can say then that thin lenses give sharp images of far away things, while thick lenses give sharp images of near things.

11.7 THE FOCUSING CAMERA

Experiment 11.6
How a lens focuses on close and distant objects

In a camera the lens is made of glass and, of course, its shape cannot change.

The room should be dimmed. Put the light bulb 200 cm from the screen and move the lens until you get a sharp picture on the screen.

Measure the distance from the lens to the screen and make a note of it. Now place the bulb 50 cm from the screen and again move the lens until the picture becomes sharp. Measure this distance from the lens to the screen.

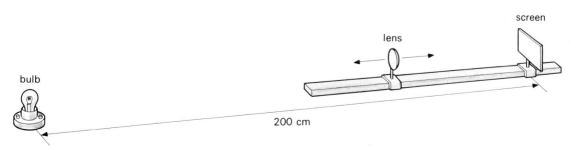

Fig. 11.8

You should have found that when the bulb was in the second position, the lens had to be moved further away from the screen than in the first position.

This is how a camera is focused. To take a clear picture of a close object the lens has to be moved outwards towards the object. The lens has to be moved inwards towards the back of the camera to focus on a distant object.

You can test what you found out about focusing with a lens in the last experiment by trying the next experiment on an old focusing camera, perhaps of the bellows type shown in Fig. 11.9.

Experiment 11.8
Finding the focal length of a lens

This experiment is also best done in a dimmed room. Adjust a power pack to 12 volts and connect the output to a ray box. Place the ray box on a sheet of white paper. Switch on the power pack and adjust the ray box so that three parallel rays are made. Place a convex lens of the type shown in the diagram in the path of the rays. Do you see that if you place this lens correctly the rays come together (**converge**)?

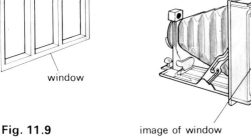

camera with back removed and replaced by greaseproof paper screen

window

image of window

Fig. 11.9

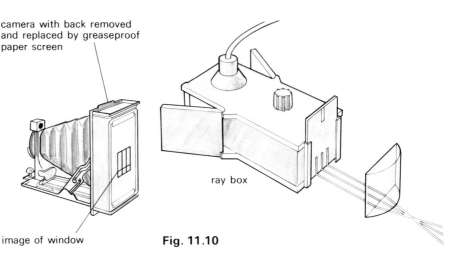

ray box

Fig. 11.10

Experiment 11.7
Focusing a camera

Darken the room, leaving only one window without the blinds down. Now open up the camera and put a piece of greaseproof paper at the back where the film would be. It can be held in position by a piece of sticky tape. Put the shutter to B, open the shutter, and point the lens at the window. Adjust the camera lens until the window frame is sharply focused on the paper screen. You can put a cloth or a jacket over your head so that you can see the image more clearly.

Now adjust the lens so that the objects outside the room are in sharp focus. Is the window frame still sharp on the screen? Have you had to move the lens inwards this time? Do you agree with the rule given at the end of the last experiment?

The point where the rays cross over is called the **focus.** Mark this point on the paper with a pencil and then draw round the lens. The distance from the focus to the centre of the lens is called the **focal length**. Ask your teacher to which part of the lens you should measure, as this can vary for different shapes of lens. Measure the focal length of the lens you have used.

Replace the lens you have just used with a more rounded convex lens and find its focal length in the same way. Which of the two lenses has the shorter focal length?

The thinner and less curved lenses do not usually make rays converge quickly and have a long focal length. The thicker and more curved lenses usually make rays converge more quickly and have a shorter focal length.

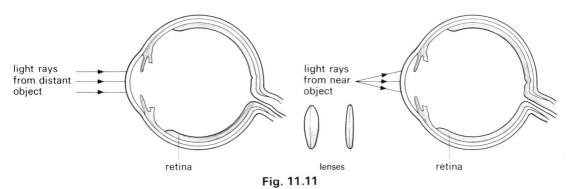

Fig. 11.11

11.8 HOW THE EYE LENS FOCUSES

Which of the lenses in Fig. 11.11 would be needed to bring the rays of light from a distant object to a point on the retina? Which one would focus the rays from a near object?

Like the bullock's eye, our eyes can change their shape. The ability of the eye lens to change its shape is called **accommodation**. The change is made by muscles like those you saw in the dissected eye. The lens is made thick with a short focal length to focus close objects, and thin with a long focal length to focus distant objects.

Hold your thumb about 30 cm in front of you and close one eye. With the other eye stare at the thumb so that you can see it in sharp focus. Does the background appear blurred? Now focus on an object in the background. Is the thumb blurred now? Using this one eye switch from the thumb to the background, back and forward, a number of times. Is your eye feeling sore? This happens because the focusing muscles in your eye are getting a little tired.

Experiment 11.9
Defects in vision: how glasses help

Some boys and girls cannot see clearly without glasses. The lens in their eye cannot focus an image correctly on the retina. This may be because the distance between the lens and the retina is either too small or too large.

You need a flask like the one in Fig. 11.12. It has different lenses attached to it. Fill the flask with water to which a little fluorescein has been added. This makes it possible to see rays passing through the water. Shine parallel rays of light from a ray box onto the flask. Rotate the flask to see how each of the lenses affects the beam of light.

The flask and lens is a model eye. The far side of the flask represents the retina, and one of the lenses should focus the light onto it. This is just what happens in an eye with good vision. The lens which brings the light to

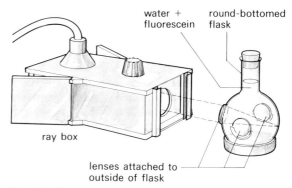

Fig. 11.12

a focus in front of the 'retina' shows what happens when a person is short sighted. Find a lens to put in front of the model eye which corrects this and throws the point at which the rays converge (the focus point) exactly on to the 'retina'. What kind of lens is it – concave or convex?

The lens which brings the light to a focus behind the 'retina' shows what happens when a person is long sighted. Find out what kind of lens is needed to correct this and bring the rays to a focus on the retina.

If there are boys and girls in your class who wear glasses, ask them if you may find out whether they are long or short sighted. You should now be able to do this just by feeling the lenses in their glasses.

Remember that a convex lens is thicker in the middle than at the edges. You should have just found that this is the type of lens needed to correct long sight. A concave lens, which is thinner in the middle than at the edges, is used to correct short sight.

11.9 THE RETINA

It has been found that there are different kinds of sensitive cells on the retina. One kind is called a 'rod' because of its shape. The rods are sensitive to white light or to the absence of light (that is, blackness). Others are called 'cones', also because of their shape. They are triggered off by lights of different colours.

11.10 COLOUR BLINDNESS

In about one in twelve males not all the cones function properly. These people have difficulty telling the difference between red and green things. They are called colour blind. People who are colour blind need not feel upset – there must be over two million others like them in Great Britain alone. Such people, however, cannot do a job in which it is necessary to distinguish between colours. These include becoming an aircraft pilot, a railway engine driver, a ship's officer, and an electrician.

Experiment 11.10
Are you colour blind?

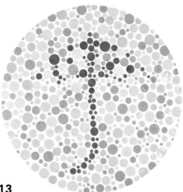

Fig. 11.13

Test each other with special colour blindness test cards. How many boys in the class are colour blind? How many girls?

11.11 VISION

Experiment 11.11
Can you judge distance with one eye?

In this simple experiment you should work with a partner. He or she should stand facing you, about four or five paces away, with a hand stretched out and the first finger pointing straight up.

Stretch out one hand with your first finger pointing straight down. Close one eye, walk slowly towards your partner, and try to place your downwards pointing finger directly on top of the finger your partner is pointing upwards. Can you do this easily? You will probably

Fig. 11.14

either stab your finger down in front of your partner's or behind it. It is very difficult to judge distance accurately using only one eye.

Now go back five paces from your partner and repeat the experiment keeping both eyes open. Do you find it difficult to place your finger accurately this time?

It is clearly much easier to judge distance using both eyes. Sportsmen who have lost the use of an eye find ball games much more difficult as they need both eyes to locate exactly where the ball is. Wild animals which prey on others for food have both eyes directed forwards so that they can judge the distance to their prey exactly.

Here is another little experiment very much like the last one. Close one eye and hold a pen at arm's length. Now try to fit the cap on the pen with the other hand, keeping one eye closed.

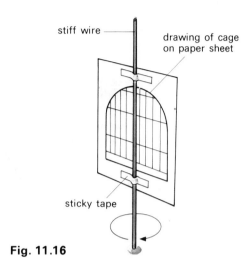

stiff wire

drawing of cage on paper sheet

sticky tape

Fig. 11.16

Experiment 11.12
Finding your angle of vision

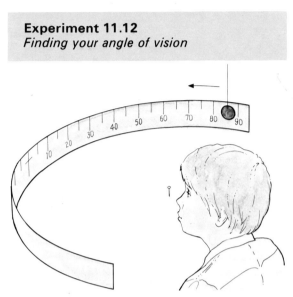

Fig. 11.15

If you do this extra experiment you will need a partner. Support the curved strip of material in a semi-circle at the edge of the bench as shown in the diagram. Place your nose at the pin and look steadily at the cross where the zero on the scale is. Ask your partner to move the black card circle along the strip from one end as in Fig. 11.15. As soon as you notice the card out of the corner of your eye, tell your partner to stop, and to note this angle on the scale.

Repeat this experiment with other card circles of different sizes and of different colours. Note the angle in each case. Is the angle always the same? Can you always say what the colour is when you first see the card?

Take a sheet of stiff drawing paper about 15 cm square. On one side draw a bird or an animal and on the other side draw a fairly large cage with quite widely spaced bars as in Fig. 11.16. Now stick a fairly stiff piece of wire – a long knitting needle will do – down the centre of one side of the paper. Spin the needle very quickly between your hands. What do you see? Has the bird or animal got into the cage?

You should have found that you are not usually aware of colour at the edge of your view of things. Did you see the yellow cards most quickly? Most people do.

What colour of car do you think is most easily seen by a motorist on the road? What colour are school buses in America and Telecom vans in this country? Can you say why this colour might have been chosen?

If you have an old note book, you can make a series of 'match-stick men' drawings in the top corner of each page. Each time draw the limbs in a slightly different position. When you flick the pages over quickly it will look as if the man is moving. With a little practice you can draw pictures of cats chasing mice, people running and jumping, and so on, which will seem to move smoothly when you flick over the pages.

Have you ever seen a reel of cine film? About 24 pictures are flashed onto the screen every second, but we do not see them as 24 separate still pictures. Our eyes blend one image into the next as the nerve endings on the retina retain the light signal for a short time. If you look steadily at a lamp and then switch it off you will sometimes still see a faint image of it. This is called **persistence of vision**.

11.12 SOUND AND HEARING

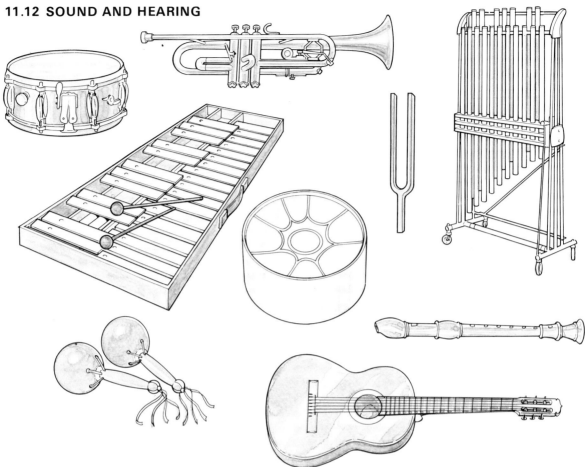

Fig. 11.17 Some musical instruments.

Experiment 11.14
Making a variety of sounds

Each member of the class should bring to school an instrument or object which can produce sounds. Exchange them among the members of the class. As well as trying some of the more expensive musical instruments, do the following simple experiments.

Fig. 11.18

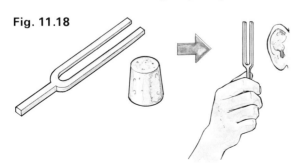

Tap a tuning fork against the heel of your shoe or on a cork and hold its end near your ear. What do you find?

Tap the fork again and touch the surface of the water lightly with one prong. What do you see on the water surface?

Tap the fork a third time and hold it lightly to your lips. What do you feel?

Fig. 11.19

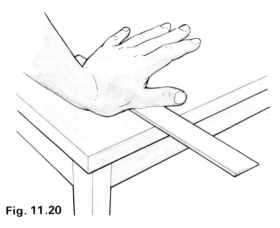

Fig. 11.20

Hold a ruler as shown in Fig. 11.20 and twang the end. Do you hear a sound? Change the length of ruler sticking out over the bench. Twang the end of the ruler again. What happens this time? Can you see the ruler moving?

The movements were more easy to see when you used the longer length of ruler. These movements are called **vibrations,** and the vibrations produce the sounds you heard. Can you now say what was vibrating in each of the instruments brought to school for this lesson?

11.13 TRANSMISSION OF SOUND

Experiment 11.15
What can sound travel through?

Ask your partner to rub the bench with one finger. Can you hear the sound when you are sitting normally at the bench? Put one ear down on the bench and put a finger in the other ear. Can you hear the rubbing now? What has the sound travelled through to reach your ear?

Fig. 11.21

For the second experiment connect a buzzer to about 6 volts from a power pack and lower the buzzer,

Fig. 11.22

wrapped in polythene, into a basin of water. Put the end of a stethoscope just under the water as in Fig. 11.22. Can you hear the sound of the buzzer travelling through the water?

You have already found that sound from a tuning fork can travel through the air. From the simple experiments you have just done you have learnt that sound vibrations can pass through solids, liquids, and gases.

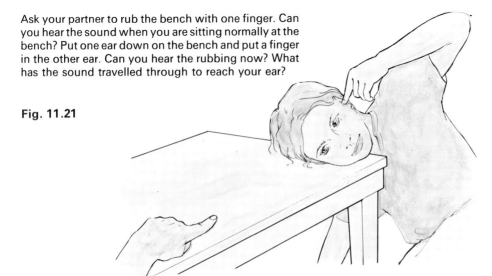

Fig. 11.23

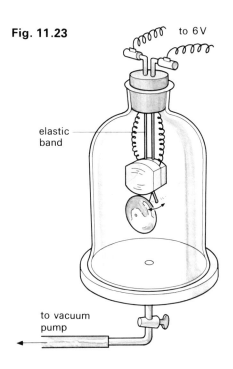

to 6 V

elastic
band

to vacuum
pump

Fit up the apparatus shown in Fig. 11.23. When the current is switched on, you should see the hammer of the bell vibrating and you should also be able to hear the sound made by the gong as it is hit. Now switch on the vacuum pump so that it begins to remove the air from the bell jar. What do you notice?

Can you still see the hammer vibrating? What happens to the strength of the sound you hear? If you have a good pump it should be able to remove practically all the air. Do not put your head too close to the bell jar. Can you hear any sound at all?

Now switch off the pump and slowly turn the screw which lets air back into the bell jar. What happens?

You have discovered that sound does not travel in a vacuum. This is clearly different from light and from heat waves, which reach us from the Sun. To do this they have to pass through empty space. There may be huge explosions taking place on the Sun but the noise of them would never reach us because there is a vacuum between us and the Sun, and, as Experiment 11.16 has shown, sound cannot travel through a vacuum.

It is interesting to think about the Moon which has no air round it and so exists in total silence.

Astronauts on the Moon had to talk to each other by radio. How could two astronauts on the Moon talk to each other if their radios had broken down? Perhaps they could lean towards each other so that their space helmets touch and the sound vibrations could then pass from one to the other.

11.14 THE EAR

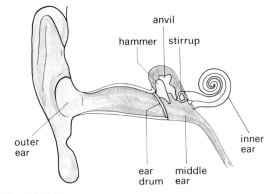

anvil

hammer   stirrup

outer
ear

inner
ear

ear   middle
drum   ear

Fig. 11.24

Look at the diagram of an ear in Fig. 11.24. You will see that there are three regions.

(a) The **outer ear** is a flap to catch sound vibrations, and a tube. The vibrations are guided down the tube onto the ear drum. Some animals can move their ear flaps to pick up sound from different directions; you have probably noticed a dog or a cat doing this.

(b) The **middle ear**. This area acts as a kind of lever.

From Fig. 11.25 you will see that a small movement of the short end of a lever causes a big movement of the other end of the lever. In the same way, the bones in the middle ear make the vibrations of the ear drum bigger before they pass on to the inner ear. In other words the middle ear acts as an amplifier. The three bones, the **hammer**, the **anvil**, and the **stirrup** were named after the things their shapes remind us of. They are the smallest bones in our bodies.

A tube leads from the middle ear to the back of the throat. When we swallow, some air leaves this tube and we hear a 'click' as the air round about pushes our ear drums in. Try listening for this little noise in your ear when you swallow.

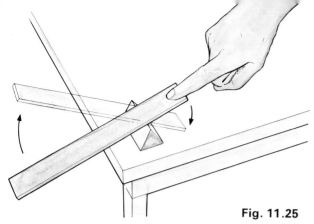

Fig. 11.25

(c) The **inner ear** looks like a snail's shell and is called the **cochlea**. It contains nerve endings which each pick out different sounds. The nerves lead from the cochlea to the brain.

If any one of these three parts of the ear is damaged, deafness can result. That is why you should not push any object into your ear, or blow your nose too hard. Which parts of the ear might you damage if you do?

Experiment 11.17
More experiments with tuning forks

(a) High and low notes

Look closely at a variety of tuning forks of different lengths. Can you see a number stamped on each fork? Do you know what this number means? It tells you the number of vibrations the fork makes in one second. This is called the **frequency**, and is measured in units called **hertz** (Hz for short).

Tap the short fork on your heel or a cork and then either hold it to your ear or press the handle onto the bench. Repeat this with a long fork. Which fork makes the higher note? Which fork has the higher frequency?

You should find that the short fork has the higher frequency and gives a high note, while the long fork has the lower frequency and gives a low note.

Have you come across a fork with 440 Hz marked on it? This fork gives the musical note 'A' to which all orchestras and groups tune their instruments. After the last TV programmes have finished, this note is broadcast to wake people who have fallen asleep in front of their sets!

(b) Making the sound louder

Tap a fork and hold it near your ear. Tap it again and press the end of the handle on a hollow box. Is the sound as loud as it was before? Why is there this big difference? What is in the hollow box? What happens to all this air when the handle of the tuning fork is pressed onto the box?

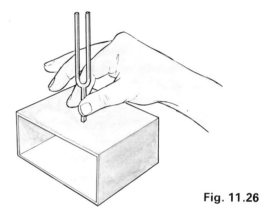

Fig. 11.26

Many musical instruments make use of the fact that hollow containers can amplify sound. Write down the name of as many as you can.

Experiment 11.18
The signal generator

The apparatus is shown in Fig. 11.27. The **signal generator** is connected up to a **cathode ray oscilloscope** (c.r.o.) and to a loudspeaker. When the tuning knob of the generator is turned clockwise the pointer

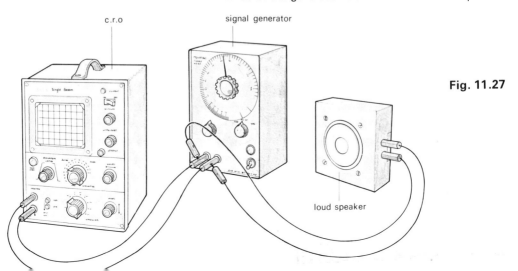

c.r.o

signal generator

Fig. 11.27

loud speaker

travels up the frequency scale and the note from the loudspeaker becomes higher. This generator can produce a wider range of frequencies than any of the instruments you have come across in this section.

Your teacher will help you to set up the oscilloscope. When it has been adjusted correctly, switch on the generator. You should be able to see a pattern of **waves** on the oscilloscope screen. When you increase the frequency of the signal generator what do you notice happening to the length of the waves on the screen? What happens to the note from the loudspeaker?

Increasing the frequency should make all the waves on the screen crowd together so that each complete wave is shorter from left to right.

The distance between one wave and the next, where it exactly repeats itself, is called the **wavelength**. The principle of the signal generator is used in constructing electronic organs.

Experiment 11.19
What is the highest note you can hear?

Do you think you can hear the whole range of notes that the signal generator can produce? You can find out by adjusting the volume control to a suitable level, putting the frequency controls to the bottom of the scale, and then slowly increasing the frequency. What do you notice on the oscilloscope screen? During the experiment you will probably need your teacher's help in adjusting the oscilloscope.

Depending upon how good your loudspeaker is, some of you might just be able to hear a very low note as the generator reading reaches about 20 Hz. Below this you are unlikely to hear any note at all — only a series of pops.

As you increase the frequency, you should again see the waves on the screen becoming shorter and shorter while the note from the speaker gets higher and higher. What is the frequency of the very highest note you can hear? To check that there really *are* vibrations coming from the generator, the **time base** control of the c.r.o. will probably have to be adjusted to its fastest setting.

Now repeat the experiment, but this time set the generator to its highest frequency on the scale. Of course, this will produce a note which it too high for you to hear. Gradually reduce the frequency until you can hear a very high whistle. How does this compare with the frequency of the highest note you heard when you were increasing the frequency?

If you do this experiment with a large group of pupils you will find that not all pupils hear the same highest note. Some will not hear a note higher than 16000 Hz while others will be able

to hear a note at 19000 Hz. As we get older, the highest note we can hear gets lower. Older people might not be able to hear the squeak of a mouse, whereas you can. Many animals, such as dogs for example, are able to hear much higher notes than humans. This might be very important for their own safety.

Try to find out how a bat uses its sense of hearing to enable it to fly safely in darkness.

11.15 HOW SOME MUSICAL INSTRUMENTS WORK

Experiment 11.20
Stringed instruments

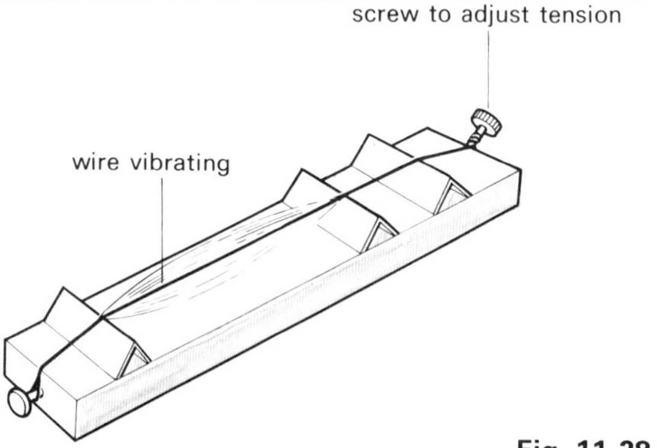

Fig. 11.28

Can you name some stringed instruments? Look at a piece of apparatus called a **sonometer**. It is simply a wire stretched along a hollow box. Pluck the string. What happens to the string? The vibrating string gives a particular note. What happens to this note when you move the bridge away from the end? The length of wire which is vibrating becomes shorter and the note sounds higher because these vibrations are faster. Slide the bridge back to the end, pluck the string, and again listen to the note. Now turn the screw clockwise just a little. This makes the string tighten. Pluck the string again without changing its length. What happens to the note this time?

Most stringed instruments are first tuned by tightening the strings to give the correct notes. You can then make lots of other notes by varying the lengths of the strings which are allowed to vibrate. This is usually done by pressing the strings with your fingers. If members of the class who play stringed instruments bring their instruments to school, perhaps they will show you how to tune and play them.

Experiment 11.21
Wind instruments

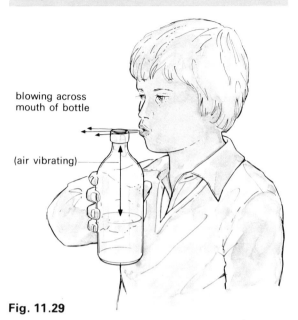

blowing across
mouth of bottle

(air vibrating)

Fig. 11.29

Blow across the top of an empty bottle. Now add a little water so that there is less air in the bottle. Blow across the top again. Is the note the same as before? You may be able to make a musical scale if you can get a set of eight test-tubes and fill them with different amounts of water. The shorter the length of the air, the higher the note produced as the air vibrates.

'Wind' instruments work in the same way as the bottle. Perhaps someone in the class can demonstrate how a recorder is played. When all the air holes are covered up, the whole length of air inside the tube vibrates. When you remove a finger and uncover a hole, the length of air which is actually vibrating is shortened and so the note rises.

Fig. 11.30 Playing a recorder.

11.16 SOME THINGS TO DO AT HOME

1 You need two empty tins. Make sure that there are no jagged edges at the open end. With a nail, knock a hole in the bottom of each can and thread a long piece of string through the holes so that the cans are bottom to bottom.

Now tie a knot at each end of the string so that the cans will not become unthreaded. Ask a friend to hold one tin to his or her ear and walk away until the string is tight. Then, keeping the string very tight, speak into the other tin. Keep the tins in line with the string for best results.

2 Fill a plastic bag or a rubber balloon with water. Hold this to your ear and place a ticking watch on the other side of the bag. Can you hear the sound from the watch passing through the water?

3 Put one ear close to a metal fence, a railing, or a pipe in a central heating system. Ask someone to tap or rub the metal some distance away from you with a screwdriver. Can you hear anything?

4 Uncoil a hosepipe and stretch it out as far as it will go without any wrinkles in it. Place one end to your ear while someone whispers into the other end.

Before the telephone was invented people often used 'speaking tubes' if they wanted to talk to someone at the other end of a large house, for example. Your hosepipe is a sort of 'speaking tube'.

In all these experiments, how did the sound energy reach your ear?

11.17 TASTE, SMELL, AND OTHER SENSES

You have now studied two of your senses, sight and hearing. In Unit 1 you found that by looking at 'optical illusions', you could easily be fooled into seeing things that are not really as they seem. You have also found that you cannot hear certain sounds, although other animals are able to hear them. Does this mean that our other senses, our sense of taste, of smell, and of touch, are also easily fooled? Can we really rely on them? Does the whole surface of our tongue detect the taste of the food we eat? Do we use our noses just to smell things or do we use them to help us to taste? Do all parts of our skin feel touch, heat, and cold equally well? These are some of the problems you are now going to try to find answers to.

11.18 THE SENSE OF TASTE

Experiment 11.22
Your tongue and taste

Look carefully at your partner's tongue. Is it smooth or rough? Figure 11.31 shows the surface of the tongue, greatly enlarged.

Fig. 11.31 Electronmicrograph of the surface of the tongue (×25).

The many lumps that you can see contain nerve endings. These particular nerve endings can detect taste, and so we call them **detectors**. Although our food has many flavours, our tongue can only detect four basic tastes. These are sweet, sour, bitter, and salt. Can you tell one taste from the others?

Your teacher will set out four bottles labelled A, B, C, and D. Each contains a liquid with a different taste. Using a clean dropper, put a drop of liquid from bottle A onto your tongue. Does it taste sweet, sour, bitter, or salt? Rinse your mouth with water, and in a similar way taste the other liquids in turn. Remember to use a clean dropper each time.

You should have been able to detect each taste quite easily. Look again at the lumps on the tongue shown in Fig. 11.31.

Do you think that each of these lumps can detect all four tastes equally well, or are some more sensitive to certain tastes than others? Here is an experiment which will help you find out. You will need to work with a partner.

Experiment 11.23

Ask your partner to sit with eyes closed and tongue out. Using a *clean* dropper, take a few drops of one of the liquids used in the last experiment (Experiment 11.22), but do not say which one you have chosen. Place a drop

Fig. 11.32

of the liquid on the front of your partner's tongue as in Fig. 11.32. Ask him or her to tell you which taste it is, while the tongue is still out. Enter your result in a table like the one below. Put a tick in the appropriate box if the taste is named correctly, and a cross if the answer is wrong.

Region of mouth	Sweet	Sour	Salt	Bitter
Front				
Side				
Back				

Now test the sides and back of your partner's tongue with the same liquid. Test the three regions of the tongue with each liquid. Remember that the mouth must be rinsed out before a new liquid is added.

Figure 11.33 is a map of the tongue, showing the different regions of taste.

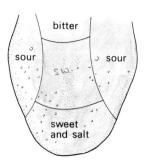

back of tongue

bitter

sour

sour

sweet and salt

Fig. 11.33   front of tongue

Draw an outline of the tongue and map your regions of taste. Is your diagram similar to that in Fig. 11.33? If it is not exactly the same do not worry – you know by now how much we vary from each other.

Experiment 11.24

You will be given two different liquids, A and B. Using a clean dropper, put a drop of liquid A onto your tongue. What taste does it have? With another clean dropper, try the taste of liquid B. Now *quickly* taste liquid A again. Does it have the same taste as before?

You probably found that your tongue was unable to taste liquid A clearly the second time, although you could taste it before liquid B had been on your tongue. Liquids A and B were similar in taste, but B was much stronger than A. Strong tastes deaden your taste detectors. As a result you have difficulty in tasting milder foods eaten soon after strong ones. If you have the choice of eating melon followed by a chicken curry, or chicken curry followed by melon, which would you choose, and why? Cigarette smoke has a strong taste and so it deadens the detectors in the tongue. People who smoke heavily do not taste their food as well as non-smokers.

Experiment 11.25

Dip a cotton bud into a strong sugar solution. Touch your tongue with the bud. Rinse out your mouth with water. Add 20 cm³ of water to the sugar solution. Taste the weaker solution. Is it different from the first solution? Add another 20 cm³ of water, and taste the solution again. Can you still detect the sugary taste? Keep adding 20 cm³ of water and tasting your mixture until it does not taste of sugar anymore. How much water did you add? Did your partner have to add the same amount of water before the taste disappeared? If not, can you explain why?

Why do you think you could not taste the sugar after the solution had been diluted? Our tongues can only detect a taste if it is strong enough. Very weak tastes are difficult to detect.

11.19 TASTE AND SMELL

Experiment 11.26

This experiment will probably be pleasant to do because you are going to eat crisps.
   Your teacher will give you three dishes of crisps marked A, B, and C. Do not eat them all before you do the experiment! Close your eyes. Hold a crisp from dish A to your nose, then eat a crisp from dish B. What flavour was the crisp you ate? Again hold a crisp from dish A to your nose and this time eat a crisp from dish C. What flavour of crisp did you eat this time? Take crisp A away from your nose. Now taste crisps B and C. What

Fig. 11.34

flavour are they? What two senses do we need to use to detect accurately the flavours of our food? Why do we have difficulty in tasting food when we have a bad cold?

11.20 THE SENSE OF SMELL

When we taste the flavour of food we use both our tongue and our nose. The lining of our nose is moist. Gases can dissolve in this layer of moisture. When they do, they are sensed by detectors at the back of the nose. The detectors contain nerve endings. Figure 11.35 shows you where these detectors are found.

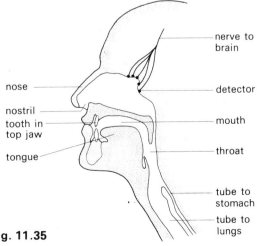

Fig. 11.35

Fig. 11.36

Experiment 11.27

Smell the strong coffee in the bottle provided. Close one nostril, hold the bottle under your nose and breathe in through your open nostril. Breathe out through your mouth. Did you smell the coffee? Repeat this many times. What happens to the smell of coffee? Is there still coffee in the bottle? Why has the smell of coffee disappeared?

If you continue to sniff something strong, the detectors in your nose become less sensitive to that smell. As a result you become less and less aware of the smell, until in the end it cannot be detected.

11.21 THE SENSE OF TOUCH

The last sense organ to investigate is our skin. Skin covers the entire surface of our body and it carries out a number of very important functions. It protects our internal organs; it holds us together; and it helps us to be aware of our surroundings. Skin helps us to feel objects; to recognize their texture, size, and shape; and to tell our body whether an object is hot or cold.

The following experiments will show you how you use your skin as a sense organ.

Experiment 11.28
Touch

Close your eyes and ask your partner to touch your hand. Tell him or her when you feel your hand being touched.

Experiment 11.29
Texture

Put your hand into the bag provided and feel the three squares. Pick out the smoothest one, and then pick out the roughest.

Experiment 11.30
Shape

Fig. 11.37

Put on a blindfold. Your partner will give you a piece of card with cut out letters on it. The letters form a message. Using only your fingers, 'read' the instructions written on the card, then carry them out.

Experiment 11.31
Temperature

Put on a blindfold. Your partner will give you two beakers A and B. Beaker A contains warm water and B contains cold water. Using only your fingertips find out which is beaker A and which is beaker B.

What do you think is present in your skin to enable you to be aware of touch, texture, and temperature?

You have discovered that all of our other sense organs have limitations. Our eyes can be deceived, our ears cannot hear certain sounds, our tongues can only detect certain tastes in certain regions. Is our skin limited in what it feels? Do we feel objects equally well with all parts of our skin? Is the whole surface of our skin sensitive to hot and cold, or are some areas more sensitive than others? Let us find out.

Experiment 11.32

Close your eyes. Your partner has two pieces of paper. One is rough and the other is smooth. He or she will touch your fingertips, first with one piece, then with the other. You must decide which one is the rough piece. In the same way, find out whether the skin on the back of your hand, on the back of your neck, and on your forearm can distinguish between the rough paper and the smooth paper.

Experiment 11.33
Which part of your skin is most sensitive?

Your teacher will give you a stamp with a pattern of dots on it. Press the stamp firmly onto an ink pad. Now press it onto the back of your partner's hand. There should now be a copy of the dots on the back of his or her hand. Stamp the same pattern in your notebook. Dip a thin, blunt, metal rod into a beaker of hot water until it becomes warm. *Carefully touch* one of the dots on your partner's skin. If the rod feels warm to your partner put a tick on the same dot on the pattern you have stamped in your notebook. If he or she just feels the sensation of touch, do not mark that dot. Do this for each dot in the pattern. Now repeat the experiment, but this time put the rod into ice cold water. Put crosses on the dots where a cold spot is felt. Do you feel hot and cold sensations equally well all over your skin?

As a result of all your experiments on skin you should have found that skin contains detectors which are sensitive to touch. These detectors contain nerve endings. Our finger tips contain many of these detectors grouped closely together. They are spread further apart in the skin on the back of the neck. Your skin also contains detectors which are sensitive to heat and to cold. You could only feel heat when a hot rod was placed near to one of these heat detectors, and cold when a cold rod was placed near to a cold detector. When the rod was placed too far from these nerve endings, you felt only the sensation of touch.

In Unit I (Experiment 1.5) you found that your skin could not measure the temperature of water accurately. Your idea of how hot or cold an object was seemed to depend on the temperature of the object you had touched just beforehand. Again we see that our sense organs can be easily fooled.

11.22 USING OUR SENSES

Your senses form just one part of a highly complicated and very wonderful system called the **nervous system**. Let us see how this system works. Read the following instruction and then carry it out.

Pick up a pencil from your desk.

How has your nervous system acted to carry out this instruction? Your **eyes** looked at the pencil. Nerve endings in the **detectors** in your eyes carried the information to a **nerve**. The nerve carried the information to your **brain**. Your brain interpreted the information, i.e. it 'saw' the pencil. Your brain then sent a new lot of information by a **different nerve** to the **muscles** of your hand and arm. Your muscles moved the bones in your hand and arm and you picked up the pencil.

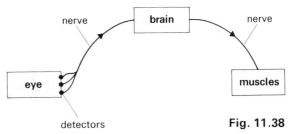

Fig. 11.38

All of our sense organs send information to the brain in this way. We are made aware of our environment and of any changes that may take place in it. Our brain interprets the information and causes our body to act accordingly. Our brain is an extremely efficient organ but, as you have found out, it can have difficulty in interpreting certain signals. Here are some more experiments to 'fool' you.

Experiment 11.34

Fig. 11.39

Shut your eyes. Feel the marble with your fingers crossed. What do you think you feel?

Experiment 11.35

Fig. 11.40

Blindfold your partner. Spin him or her round a few times. Can your partner now walk in a straight line?

Experiment 11.36

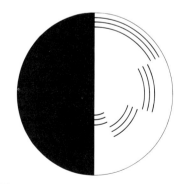

Fig. 11.41

Look at the disc. Now look at the disc spinning. What differences do you see?

Fig. 11.42

Experiment 11.37

Hold a paper tube – the centre of a kitchen towel roll will do – closely against your right eye. With *both* eyes *open* look down the tube. Now bring your left hand, with the palm facing towards your face, alongside the tube. What do you see in the centre of your palm?

11.23 CONSCIOUS AND REFLEX ACTIONS

Compare the following two incidents.

1 Two children want to cross a busy road. They start to cross, but see a car in the distance. They stop, go back onto the pavement, wait until the car passes, then cross the road.

2 Two children are running along a pavement chasing a ball. The ball goes onto the road. One child runs after the ball, without waiting to look for traffic. He is suddenly aware that a car is driving towards him. He immediately pulls back.

In the first incident, all the children's actions were **conscious actions** and occurred as a result of **thought**. The children controlled all their movements. In the second incident the boy did not wait to think 'a car is coming, I had better not go onto the road'. He automatically jumped back onto the pavement when he saw a car. His actions were very rapid and helped him to escape injury. His brain was not used to process the information. This type of action is called a **reflex action**.

We have a number of reflex actions, most of which we were born with. These actions are very quick, and usually help us to escape injury. We blink if a bright light is shone into our eyes. We sneeze if something irritates our nose. Can you think of any more reflex actions?

11.24 REACTION TIMES

Have you ever heard anyone say 'I have done that so often that I can do it without thinking'? If we repeat a particular action many, many times we can complete it faster, and our brain may no longer be required to control the action. The action becomes a reflex action.

Experiment 11.38
Reaction times

The stick used in this experiment has a special scale marked on it. Your partner will hold the stick above your hand. Place your thumb and finger around the base of the stick, but do not touch it. When your partner lets it go, catch the stick and hold it firmly. What number on

Fig. 11.43

the scale is your finger touching? Let us suppose that the number is 0.20. This means that it has taken you 0.2 s to catch the stick. Your reaction time for this catch is 0.2 s. Repeat this experiment ten times, and each time record how long it took you to catch the stick. Draw a graph of your results. Is your reaction time affected by practice?

11.25 THE BRAIN

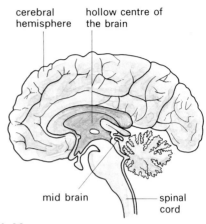

cerebral hemisphere — hollow centre of the brain

mid brain — spinal cord

Fig. 11.44

Figure 11.44 shows an outline of the human brain. The brain contains millions of nerve cells. These are very special cells. Some of them receive information from our sense organs and interpret it; some send messages to move our muscles; some control our breathing and our heart beat; some store information and act as our memory; some give us imagination and others enable us to think. The brain is a very wonderful organ.

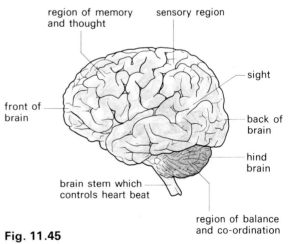

region of memory and thought — sensory region

front of brain

brain stem which controls heart beat

sight

back of brain

hind brain

region of balance and co-ordination

Fig. 11.45

Figure 11.45 shows a map of the brain. From it find the part which
(a) controls memory and thought;
(b) controls breathing and heart beat;
(c) receives messages from the eyes;
(d) controls our balance and co-ordination.

WHAT YOU HAVE LEARNT IN THIS UNIT

1 The most important parts of the eye are the lens and the retina. The retina is the coating at the back of the eye which receives the image.

2 The convex lens in the eye focuses light onto the retina and can change its shape to do this. When focusing on objects near to the eye it becomes thicker in the middle and its focal length becomes shorter. When focusing on distant objects it becomes thinner in the middle and its focal length becomes longer. The ability of the lens in the eye to change its shape in this way is called accommodation.

3 A concave spectacle lens is needed to help people with short sight. A convex lens is needed to help people with long sight.

4 A camera works like an eye, but it focuses images of objects onto a film – the lens is moved towards or away from the film instead of changing its shape.

5 In both the eye and the camera the image formed is upside down and the wrong way round.

6 About one male in twelve cannot distinguish easily between the colours red and green. He is said to be colour blind.

7 The colour yellow is more easily seen at a wide angle than other colours.

8 Two eyes are better than one at judging distance.

9 Our eyes can often play tricks on us. This happens when the brain does not interpret messages correctly.

10 Sounds are produced as a result of vibrations.

11 The smallest bones in our bodies are in the middle ear. Their job is to make sound vibrations bigger.

12 A slow rate of vibration gives a low note; a fast rate of vibration gives a high note. The number of vibrations per second is called the frequency of the vibrations and is measured in hertz (Hz).

13 The range of notes we hear is limited. As we grow older we cannot hear such high notes as we could when we were young.

14 Long vibrating wires and tubes of air produce low notes; short ones produce high notes.

15 Sound vibrations require particles to pass them on. These vibrations can pass through solids, liquids, and gases, but not through a vacuum because there are no particles in a vacuum.

16 There are four basic tastes, sweet, sour, salt, and bitter, which can be detected by nerve endings in the tongue.

17 Detectors in different regions of the tongue are sensitive to different tastes. Sweet and salt are usually tasted at the front of the tongue, sour at the sides, and bitter at the back.

18 Very strong tastes can temporarily deaden taste detectors, making it difficult for you to taste milder substances.

19 Cigarette smoke deadens taste detectors as it has a strong taste.

20 The tongue can detect tastes only if they are strong enough. Very dilute substances are difficult to taste.

21 The nose contains detectors which are sensitive to smell.

22 The sense of taste and smell are closely connected. One affects the other.

23 When you continue to sniff a strong smell, the detectors in your nose become less sensitive to that smell, until finally it cannot be detected.

24 Our skin contains many detectors. Some respond to touch, some to heat, and some to cold.

25 The detectors in the skin are not distributed evenly. Our finger-tips contain many touch detectors grouped closely together, and so the tips of our fingers are very sensitive to touch.

26 We can use our skin to identify the texture and shape of objects.

27 The skin is sensitive to heat and cold only around nerve endings.

28 The skin is not accurate in judging the temperature of objects.

29 Our sense organs make us aware of any changes in our environment.

30 All signals from our sense organs are taken to the brain by nerves. The brain interprets this information. A new set of signals is sent from the brain along different nerves to certain muscles and glands, which then respond.

31 Our brain has difficulty in interpreting certain signals, and can be confused.

32 Actions controlled by the brain are called conscious actions.

33 Reflex actions are not controlled by the brain, but occur automatically. They are rapid actions which usually help us to escape injury.

34 The time that it takes for a stimulus to produce a resulting action is called the reaction time.

35 Our brain contains millions of nerve cells. It is a very complicated and wonderful organ.

NEW WORDS YOU HAVE MET IN THIS UNIT

accommodation   the ability of the eye lens to change its shape.

aperture   the opening through which light enters a camera or the eye.

aqueous humour   watery liquid in the eyeball.

blind spot   the area of the retina in which there are no light-sensitive cells because the optic nerve enters at that point.

camera   an instrument for taking photographs by focusing light onto a film.

cathode ray oscilloscope   apparatus for observing and measuring variations in voltage.

cochlea   the part of the inner ear coiled like a snail's shell.

colour blind   unable to distinguish certain colours, particularly red and green.

concave   a disc which is thicker at the edges than in the middle.

conscious action   an action controlled by thought.

converging   coming together.

convex   a disc which is thicker in the middle than at the edges.

cornea   the transparent part of the coat of the eyeball at the front of the eye.

detector   the area in a sense organ containing nerve endings.

diverge   spread out.

environment   the region round about.

focal length   the distance from the centre of a lens to its focus.

focus   the point at which rays of light are brought together by the action of a lens or spherically curved mirror.

frequency   the number of vibrations per second.

image   the picture of an object produced by a lens or a mirror.

iris   part of the eye lying in front of the lens consisting of a coloured circular area with an opening through which light enters the eye.

lens   a disc of material, usually glass or plastic, shaped so that it brings light to a focus.

nerve   a group of cells which carry impulses from one part of the body to another.

nervous system   the system which includes the brain, sense organs, and all the nerves in the body.

optic nerve   the nerve which carries messages from the retina of the eye to the brain.

persistence of vision   continuing to see an object when the light from it has been cut off.

reaction time   the time between receiving a stimulus and responding to it.

reflex action   an automatic response to a stimulus.

retina   the coating at the back of the eye composed of cells which are sensitive to light.

sclerotic coat   the tough outer coat of the eye.

sense organ   an organ of the body which receives stimuli from the environment and passes them to the brain.

signal generator   a generator of electric currents which change direction very frequently and when passed into a loud speaker produce sound waves.

sonometer   apparatus consisting of a stretched steel wire which gives a note when plucked.

vibration   a to-and-fro movement.

vitreous humour   a jelly-like substance in the eye.

wave   a crest and trough movement.

wave length   the distance between two crests or two troughs of a wave.

SOME QUESTIONS FOR YOU

Copy and complete the following sentences.

1   A lens which is thicker at the middle than at the edges is called a .... lens.
2   The coloured part of the eye is called the ....
3   To focus images of objects on the retina the lens of the eye changes its shape. To focus distant objects it gets ....; to focus near objects it gets .... This is called ....
4   A short-sighted person needs spectacles with .... lenses.
5   A person who cannot tell the difference between red and green is said to be ....
6   Sound is produced when objects ....

7   The number of vibrations per second is called the .... of the note.
8   The higher the frequency the .... is the pitch of the note.
9   We cannot control some of the things we do. These are called .... actions.
10 The time it takes for a message to travel from a receptor to the brain and back to the place where action takes place is called the ....
11 The four basic tastes are ...., ..., ..., and ....

Copy the following diagram and fill in the blanks to show the connection between some of the parts of our nervous system. The first link has been completed for you.

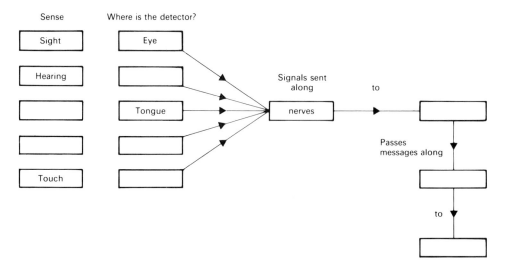

UNIT 12

The Earth

12.1 THE IMPORTANCE OF THE EARTH

In this Unit we are going to find out about the planet on which we live, and how humans have been able to get useful things from it. Have you ever thought that the Earth is our only source of metals, our only source of fuels, and our only source of food? In fact all the raw materials from which things are made come from the earth, or from the water and air round about it.

12.2 HOW IT ALL STARTED

Since no-one lived on the Earth until a very long time after it was formed, no-one knows just how it all started. To find out about the beginning, all that we can do is to look for clues among the things around us. Then we have to make guesses, and try to find the best theory to explain what we have found. You will remember that this is what you had to do when you found out about the nature of matter in Unit 4.

When we look at the Earth we find that it is made up of rocks. Some of these stick up in the form of mountains. In other places there is soil with plants growing in it. You will be looking at the soil later, but you should realize that it is made up largely of tiny pieces of rock, as well as decayed plants. In some places the rocks are covered with water. In fact water now covers about three-quarters of the surface of the Earth.

Now look at some rocks. Perhaps they will give you some clues about the way the Earth was formed.

Experiment 12.1
Looking at rocks

If you are out hill-climbing you may be able to pick up some very beautiful samples of rock. Quartz, granite, and calcite are some of them. Look at pieces of these rocks in your school collection. What do they all have in common? Try scratching them with a knife. Are they very hard? Do they dissolve in water?

Many rocks are beautiful because they are made up of crystals. This is the case for all three rocks you have just looked at. The crystals are very different in size. Those in granite are very small; calcite crystals are usually much larger. You may have to look at the granite with a hand lens to see the crystals properly.

Fig. 12.1 Crystals of (top) granite, (bottom left) calcite, and (bottom right) quartz.

In Unit 5 you learnt that crystals can be made in at least two ways. One is by the cooling of a liquid. The other is by the slow evaporation of a saturated solution.

You might like to remind yourself about the first of these ways.

Phenyl - 2 - Hydroxy benzoate .

Experiment 12.2
Making crystals of salol

Put a very little salol onto a microscope slide. Rest it on a tripod stand and warm it very gently by waving a burner with a small flame around underneath the slide. When the salol has formed a blob of liquid (i.e. when it has all melted) let it cool and look at it with a hand lens or under the low power of the microscope. You will be able to see the crystals of salol growing as the molten substance solidifies.

Fig. 12.2

You have found that quartz, granite, and calcite are insoluble in water, so it seems unlikely that the crystals of these rocks could have been made from a saturated solution. So, the clue that Experiment 12.2 gives you is that it is possible that these rocks were once molten, and formed crystals as they cooled.

Perhaps the Earth was at some time in the long distant past in a molten state. The outside cooled and the molten rocks became solid. Another reason for this idea is that, even now, the inside of the Earth is much hotter than the outside layer. The temperature in a coal mine is higher than on the surface. It is thought that the centre of the Earth is still so hot that the material there has never become solid. This is shown when volcanoes erupt and send out liquid rock in the form of lava, together with showers of ashes and jets of steam and hot water.

Fig. 12.3 A volcano during eruption.

Here is a list of volcanoes. Find out where they are from your atlas:

Etna, Vesuvius, Fujiyama, Krakatoa, Stromboli, Popocatapetl.

There are no longer any active volcanoes in Great Britain, but there is much evidence that some of the hills and mountains in this country are parts of old volcanoes. For example, the rock on which Edinburgh Castle stands is a volcanic plug – that is, the centre of the crater of an old volcano. It is harder than the rock round about which has been worn away.

Fig. 12.4 Edinburgh Castle, which is built on a volcanic plug.

Rocks which have been molten at some time are called **igneous rocks**. The word 'igneous' means 'formed by fire'. The word 'ignite', meaning 'to burn' or 'to heat', comes from the same Latin word meaning 'fire'.

There are other kinds of rocks, too. Although most rocks do not dissolve in water, the rain, frost, and wind may break them up into smaller pieces.

These are washed down by rain and by rivers until in the end they reach the sea. It is a very slow process, and it may take thousands of years for rocks to be worn down like this. This process of wearing away is called **weathering**. The tiny rock particles settle as mud, silt, and sand at the bottom of the sea, or in lakes. As the deposit gets thicker, the bottom portion is squeezed more and more by the weight of the mass on top, and becomes a hard solid. Often the particles are actually cemented together by substances produced in chemical reactions. The shells of dead sea-organisms, which are made of calcium carbonate (chalk), may form a layer on top of the mass, or between layers of it. The sea may then have changed its position so that the old sea bed became dry land; or perhaps there were movements of the earth, so that what was once the sea-floor became hills, or even mountain ranges. Rocks which have been formed by pressure in this way are called **sedimentary rocks**. They include limestone, chalk, sandstone, and shales. They have all been first laid down at the bottom of a lake or the sea.

Experiment 12.3
Sediments

Fill a large gas jar or jam jar three-quarters full of water. Mix some fine gravel, sand, and chalk together and add this to the water in the jar until the jar is nearly full. Leave the contents to settle, and note all that happens. Repeat

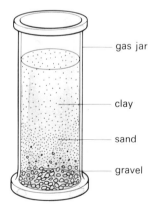

gas jar

clay

sand

gravel

Fig. 12.5

the experiment, but this time swirl the water round after adding the powdered rocks. Work out what is likely to happen when muddy water reaches the sea.

This experiment shows that sedimentary rocks are formed in layers, depending on the size of the particles and their density.

Fig. 12.6 Sedimentary rocks in Alum Bay on the Isle of Wight.

Experiment 12.4
Looking at sedimentary rocks

Look at a piece of chalk or limestone through a hand lens. Can you see any crystals there? Try scratching the rock with a knife. Is it hard or soft? What difference do you notice between chalk and granite?

Sedimentary rocks are frequently made up of rounded particles instead of crystals. They are often in layers and may contain fossils. Chalk is made of the shells of animals that once lived in the sea.

Fossils are the remains of plants or animals that lived on the Earth thousands of years ago. Their bodies were embedded in particles which became rock. Sometimes we can see the imprints of leaves of plants in pieces of coal. In some rocks you may find the remains of sea animals which were something like the present-day snails, but much larger. They are called ammonites. They had coiled shells shaped like a horn.

Fig. 12.7 Fossilized ammonites.

Fig. 12.8 Marble—a metamorphic rock—being cut from mountains in the Apuan Alps in Italy.

Fig. 12.9 A slate mine in North Wales.

Geologists – scientists who study rocks – talk of a third kind of rock called **metamorphic rocks**. This word simply means 'changed'. These rocks have been formed from other rocks by the action of heat or pressure. They may have been crushed, baked, chemically changed, and perhaps even melted. Here are the names of some metamorphic rocks: slate, schist, gneiss, quartzite, calcite, and marble. Calcite and marble are forms of calcium carbonate. They were probably once chalk or limestone, which has been changed into crystalline forms.

Experiment 12.5
Looking at metamorphic rocks

Scratch a piece of calcite or marble with a knife. Is it harder or softer than chalk? Find out whether it is more difficult to crush a piece of slate or a piece of chalk.

Slate is a hardened form of clay. Notice how it splits. It forms thin sheets and does not break up easily into powder. This makes it useful as 'slates' for the roofs of houses.

12.3 A MODEL OF THE EARTH

Figure 12.10 shows what scientists believe the structure of the Earth is like. The radius of the Earth is nearly 6000 km. The outer **crust** is very thin – only about 50 km thick. It is therefore difficult to show it to scale in a diagram. Below this thin solid crust is a soft, semi-solid **mantle**,

which is about 3000 km thick. Below this is a liquid outer **core**, and finally, at the centre, a solid inner core. The pressure at the centre of the Earth is very high because of the great mass of material above it.

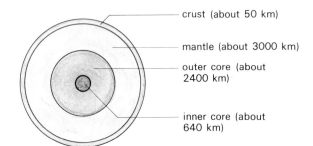

crust (about 50 km)

mantle (about 3000 km)

outer core (about 2400 km)

inner core (about 640 km)

Fig. 12.10

12.4 METALS IN NATURE

Metals are very important in everyday life. Many of the things around you are made of metal. Metals differ very much in density, in hardness, and in strength, and it is usually possible to find a metal which is right for a particular task. If we want a light but strong metal, for example to make parts of aeroplanes, we can use aluminium. If we want a metal which is hard and strong to make railway lines, for example, we can use steel, which is mainly iron.

Sometimes a mixture of metals is better for a particular purpose than a pure metal. Gold is rather soft and is easily worn away. If, however, it is mixed with copper it becomes much harder. So gold jewellery is not made of pure gold, but of a mixture of gold and copper. A mixture of metals is called an **alloy**. All the coins in your pockets are alloys, and not pure metals. The 'copper' coins are made of copper and tin. The name given to this alloy is **bronze**.

How many metals are actually found as such in nature? Not very many. Gold, silver, mercury, and platinum are found, but in very small amounts. The other metals, like magnesium, iron, aluminium, lead, zinc, copper, nickel, and chromium, never exist by themselves. They have to be extracted from rocks which contain their compounds. These compounds are called **ores**.

It is interesting to find out why these metals do not occur by themselves in nature. To do this we have to ask what other elements are present in and around the Earth. One of these is oxygen in the air, another is sulphur which is found in many parts of the earth and particularly near volcanoes, and a third is carbon, which is part of all living matter. Oxygen and sulphur in particular are very active elements, and they combine very easily with many metals. The following experiments will help to show this.

12.5 METALS AND SULPHUR

Experiment 12.6
The action of sulphur on metals

You should wear safety goggles when doing the following experiments.

(a) Mix a little of each of the following metals separately with powdered sulphur and heat each mixture in a small test-tube. Notice whether any reaction takes place and whether or not it is a strong reaction. The metals to use are iron (filings), zinc **foil** (not powdered zinc), copper foil, aluminium foil, and lead foil. Different members of the class can try different metals and you can pool your results.

(b) Get a small piece of silver foil and rub a little powdered sulphur on it.

You will have found that in many cases sulphur combines with metals. The compounds formed are called **sulphides**. Thus iron and sulphur combine together to form iron sulphide. The black stain that you get on a piece of silver foil when sulphur is rubbed on it is silver sulphide.

As you already know, there is a good deal of sulphur present in the Earth's crust. It is not surprising then that the sulphides of many metals are found in nature. Some metals are obtained from these sulphide ores.

12.6 METALS AND OXYGEN

Another very active element surrounds the Earth. It is oxygen. You already know that this gas combines very readily with some metals, although, in air, it is mixed with nitrogen which damps down its activity. Now repeat some of the experiments you did in Unit 8 to refresh your memory. Remember that in all experiments in this section you must wear safety goggles.

Experiment 12.7
The action of oxygen on metals

An easy way of finding out how well metals combine with oxygen uses the apparatus shown in Fig. 12.11.

First try heating a few crystals of potassium permanganate by themselves in a small test-tube. Hold a glowing splint at the mouth of the tube. You will remember that this is the test for oxygen. What happens? You will obtain the oxygen you need for this experiment by heating potassium permanganate crystals.

First heat the metal and then occasionally move the burner below the potassium permanganate crystals. The oxygen from the potassium permanganate passes over the heated metal. Note what happens and how vigorous the reaction is. The metals you can use are calcium turnings, magnesium ribbon (NOT powder), aluminium foil (NOT powder), zinc foil (NOT powder), lead foil, iron filings, or copper turnings. As in the last experiment, different groups of pupils can try different metals and you can pool your results.

Fig. 12.11

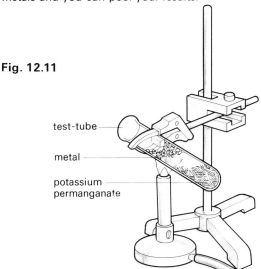

test-tube

metal

potassium permanganate

These experiments show you why the common metals do not occur by themselves in nature. It is not surprising that many ores are oxides or sulphides. These compounds are, of course, often mixed up with other minerals, and sometimes they have to be purified before we can start to get the metals from them. Here are the names of some common ores with their chemical names:

bauxite   (aluminium oxide)
haematite   (iron(III) oxide)
galena   (lead sulphide)
iron pyrites   (a sulphide of iron)
copper pyrites   (a sulphide of copper and
                   iron)
zinc blende   (zinc sulphide)

See whether these ores are in your school collection of minerals.

12.7 CARBONATES

Many common minerals are carbonates, which are compounds of a metal, carbon, and oxygen. Here are the names of some of them:

chalk
limestone
calcite   (all forms of calcium carbonate)
coral
marble
magnesite   (magnesium carbonate)
calamine   (zinc carbonate)
cerussite   (lead carbonate)
ironstone   (a carbonate of iron)

Are any of these in your school collection of minerals?

Experiment 12.8
Heating carbonates

Remember to wear safety goggles for this experiment.

(a) Heat in separate small test-tubes a little powdered chalk (natural chalk, not blackboard chalk, which is not really chalk at all), zinc carbonate, and lead carbonate. Notice everything that happens. Hold a drop of lime water on the end of a glass rod in the mouth of the tube (Fig. 12.12). What gas is given off?
(b) Hold a small piece of marble in a pair of tongs and heat it strongly (Fig. 12.13), then let it cool.
(c) While the marble is cooling, look at some zinc oxide and some lead oxide. Heat a little of the zinc oxide in a small test-tube. What happens to it? What happens when it cools down again?

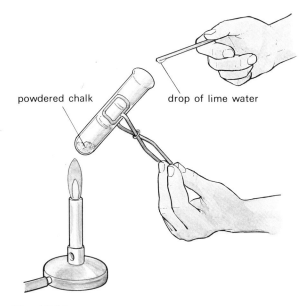

powdered chalk   drop of lime water

Fig. 12.12

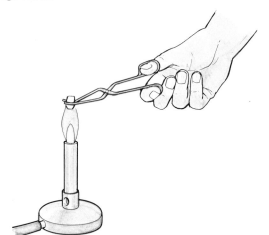

Fig. 12.13

(d) Take the product from (b) which is now cool, put it on a watch glass, and add a drop of water from a pipette dropper. What happens?
(e) Place a small piece of calcium oxide on a watch glass and add a drop of water from a dropper. What happens?

You should be able to deduce from your experiments that the carbonates you heated decompose into oxides and carbon dioxide. The word equations are:

calcium carbonate → calcium oxide
                        + carbon dioxide
zinc carbonate → zinc oxide + carbon dioxide
lead carbonate → lead oxide + carbon dioxide

Experiment 12.9
More experiments with carbonates

Different groups in the class should each take two of the following carbonates: sodium, calcium, magnesium, zinc, barium, potassium. Put a small quantity of each into a test-tube and add some dilute hydrochloric acid from a dropper. What happens?

Hold a drop of lime water on the end of a glass rod in the mouth of the test-tube. What gas is given off?

Repeat the experiment with vinegar instead of hydrochloric acid. Vinegar is dilute acetic (or ethanoic) acid.

All carbonates react with dilute hydrochloric acid and usually with other dilute acids too.

12.8 HOW ARE METALS OBTAINED FROM THEIR ORES?

We have seen that when most carbonates are heated they give off carbon dioxide and form oxides. Many sulphides also form oxides when they are heated strongly in air.

Experiment 12.10
Heating iron pyrites in air

If you look back to p. 58 you will see that iron pyrites is a sulphide of iron. Put a little heap of powdered iron pyrites onto a tin lid and heat it strongly. The tin lid may be supported on a triangle of wire placed on a tripod stand.

Can you smell a gas which is given off? What does the smell remind you of? What does the powder that is left look like?

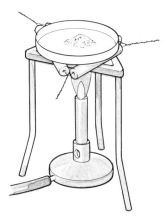

Fig. 12.14

It is thus possible to make oxides from carbonates or sulphides. As you now know, many metal ores are carbonates, sulphides, or oxides. As we can get oxides from carbonates or sulphides, the problem of getting the metal from an ore is really the problem of pulling away the oxygen from the metal oxide.

Can this be done simply by heating the oxide? You have already heated some zinc oxide. Did you get zinc from it? You have heated some carbonates and in each case one of the products was an oxide. If the oxide is broken down by heating it could not have been one of the products of this experiment. So we cannot obtain the metal just by heating the oxide.

We must look for something which has a stronger pull on oxygen than the metal has, and which can therefore split up the oxide. You already saw in Unit 10 that hydrogen is one element which has a stronger pull on oxygen than many metals have.

Another element that might also pull away the oxygen is carbon. Carbon, as you know, burns strongly in oxygen, and a great deal of energy is given out. You might expect, therefore, that carbon will pull oxygen away from some oxides. Here is an experiment to find out whether it will.

Experiment 12.11
Heating oxides with carbon

Wear protective goggles. Mix together some copper(II) oxide and some powdered charcoal. Put a small heap of the mixture onto a tin lid. Heat the mixture strongly. After a few minutes let it cool. Can you see any copper?

Repeat the experiment using lead oxide instead of copper(II) oxide. Can you see some lead?

This experiment shows that carbon *can* remove oxygen from some metal oxides. However, it cannot take oxygen from those oxides which hold onto their oxygen very strongly. Magnesium oxide, for instance, is not affected when it is heated with carbon because the magnesium combines so strongly with oxygen that neither carbon nor hydrogen can pull the oxygen away from it.

The removal of oxygen from a substance is called **reduction**; the oxide is said to be **reduced**.

12.9 MAKING IRON

One of the most important metals in the world is iron. Iron(III) oxide is heated with carbon when making iron from iron ore. The iron ore is called haematite. It is impure iron(III) oxide. It is mixed with coke (a form of carbon), and limestone, and the mixture is heated strongly in a strong blast of air in a furnace called a **blast furnace**. The limestone takes away any impurities in the ore. Molten iron is run off into sand moulds, and is usually later made into steel. The iron from the moulds is called 'pig iron'.

Fig. 12.15 A general view of the blast furnace.

Steel is made from iron by mixing a small amount of carbon with it. Steel, therefore, is impure iron. This process is done in a furnace called a **converter**.

Special kinds of steel are made for different purposes. A specially hard steel is needed to make tools, such as chisels. This hard steel is made by mixing iron with other metals such as tungsten. Stainless steel – that is, steel that will not rust – is used to make knives and forks, car bumpers, etc. It is iron alloyed with nickel and chromium.

12.10 AN INVESTIGATION OF MALACHITE

Malachite is a beautiful green mineral. It is sometimes used in jewellery, such as pendants and cuff links.

Experiment 12.12
What is malachite?

Remember to wear safety goggles.
   You should be able to find out what malachite is by yourself, but here are some hints about what to do.
(a) Try heating a little of the powdered mineral in a small test-tube. Is any gas given off? If so, what is it?
(b) Add a little dilute hydrochloric acid to some powdered malachite in a test-tube. Is any gas given off? If so, what is it?
(c) Dip a pen-knife blade, or a piece of iron rod or thick iron wire, into the solution that is left from part (b) of the experiment. What happens?
   You should now have enough information to say what malachite is.

12.11 SUBSTANCES FROM THE EARTH

Many minerals contain the element silicon. Silicon dioxide is called silica. Sand is an impure form of it.

   You have probably seen sand on the sea-shore. It is not always the same colour. This is because it is an impure form of silicon dioxide. Different impurities give it different colours. The purest form is almost white.

   When you see sand on the sea-shore you know that it has been washed many times by sea-water, yet it seems always to be the same. It does not dissolve. It is a very stable substance, and one that many substances do not attack chemically. That is why so many of our high mountains are made of compounds containing silica. They have stood for

Fig. 12.16 Molten iron being discharged at Ravenscraig, a steel works in Scotland.

Fig. 12.17 Mountains and rocks at Loch Corruisk, Isle of Skye.

Fig. 12.18 Making bricks: (a) digging out the clay; (b) grinding pans reducing the clay; (c) unfired (green) bricks ready for the kiln; (d) bricks packed into the kiln; (e) a batch of finished bricks ready for despatch; (f) a general view of the kilns and chimneys at Peterborough.

centuries without being attacked chemically by the air or by water. Substances like clay, felspar, mica, asbestos, gneiss, slate, and schists are all silicates or mixtures of silicates. Because of their great stability many of them are used for building houses.

12.12 CLAY

Clay is formed by the action of weather on granite. It is a complex silicate which contains the elements potassium and aluminium as well as silicon and oxygen. It has been used by mankind for ages. Men have built their homes out of it. The so-called 'mud huts' of primitive peoples were really made of clay which hardened in the sun to a kind of brick-like material. We still use bricks today to build our houses. Bricks are made by heating clay in a furnace. So, although bricks are easier to build with because they have a regular shape, we are not much more advanced than the primitive people who made their houses from wet clay and left it to be baked hard in the sun.

(b)

(c)

(e)

(f)

Clay has been used by potters for thousands of years to make vessels for holding solids and liquids and for making cooking utensils.

Experiment 12.13
Some experiments with clay

Roll out some potter's clay and cut it into small squares. Have some of them fired in a kiln. Leave others to dry in the open.

Describe what the clay looks and feels like before and after firing and drying.

Experiment 12.14
Glazes

Take one of the fired tiles you made in the last experiment. Dip it in salt solution and re-fire it. Examine the tile when it has cooled again. You will find that it now has a shiny surface. It looks as though it has been coated with glass. We say it has been **glazed**.

Make a glaze mixture by grinding together 2 g red lead, 2 g anhydrous sodium carbonate, 1 g powdered flint or silica, and 0.5 g cobalt(II) nitrate. Add enough water to the mixture to make a smooth paste. Paint it on one of the fired pottery tiles you made in the last experiment. Evaporate the water by gently heating the tile. Then fire the tile in the kiln, or heat it in a blowpipe flame (wear protective goggles). What colour is the glaze you get?

Other members of the class might try a glaze mixture which contains manganese(II) sulphate, iron(II) chloride, chromium(II) sulphate, or nickel(II) sulphate in place of the cobalt(II) nitrate. In this way different coloured glazes can be made.

Plates and cups and saucers are made of glazed pottery. Special kinds of clay are used to make china and porcelain. Porcelain is a very fine, thin form of china.

Other things, such as cement and concrete, are also made from clay. Cement is made by heating clay and limestone together to a very high temperature in kilns that can rotate so that the substances are always well mixed. As you know, when the limestone is heated it breaks down into carbon dioxide and calcium oxide (p. 58). Some of the calcium oxide then combines with the silicates in the clay. The resulting mixture is cement. When cement is mixed with water it sets to a hard solid after a few hours. Is this a chemical process, or does the mixture of cement and water just set to a

Fig. 12.19 A modern cement kiln.

hard lump as mud and water does? We can find out if we remember that when a chemical reaction takes place heat is either given out or taken in. Usually it is given out, and the temperature of the reacting substances rises.

Experiment 12.15
An experiment with cement

Put powdered cement into a plastic cup until it is about two-thirds full. Take the temperature of the cement. Run some tap water into a beaker and take its temperature. If the temperatures are not the same, work out the average of the two values. Now add water to the cement a little at a time, and stir until a stiff mixture is formed. Take the temperature of the mixture. Does the temperature change as the cement sets?

Do not leave the thermometer in the cement until it sets hard. It will be impossible to get it out if you do.

Concrete is made from cement mixed with gravel. Reinforced concrete is concrete moulded round a steel framework to make it stronger. Many buildings are now constructed of reinforced concrete instead of bricks or stone.

12.13 GLASS

Another very important substance made from silica is glass. Glass was probably discovered by accident when sand and soda (sodium carbonate) were heated together in a fire. The art of making, working, and colouring glass was known to the ancient Egyptians about 2000 BC.

Glass is made by melting together silica (in the form of sand or crushed quartz), calcium carbonate (limestone or chalk), and sodium carbonate. It is a complicated mixture of calcium and sodium silicates. Glass gets soft when heated and it can then be bent or shaped. As it cools it becomes hard and keeps its new shape.

Fig. 12.20 Making glass in a modern factory.

Fig. 12.21 'Blowing' glass is a skilled craft.

Glass is coloured by adding small amounts of impurities to it. Thus cobalt(II) oxide makes a beautiful dark blue glass, and copper(I) oxide a ruby red glass. The glazes you made in Experiment 12.14 were made of coloured glass.

12.14 COAL

One of the most important substances obtained from the Earth is coal. It is called a 'fossil' fuel, because it is the remains of plants which were alive on the Earth millions of years ago. These have been changed by the pressure of masses of rock lying over them. Coal probably started like peat, which is found in many British moorlands, and particularly in boggy Scottish hills where heather has changed into a dark brown or almost black mass, looking something like soil.

> **Experiment 12.16**
> *Peat*

Examine some peat and see if you can find any evidence that it has been formed from decayed vegetation. Try to burn it.

In the Highlands of Scotland, and in Ireland, peat is often burnt as a fuel. It burns slowly, and the smoke has a very pleasant smell. This peaty material became covered with rock and soil, and the pressure changed it into harder stuff. This was a kind of coal. The sort of coal formed depends on the pressure which was applied to it. Next to peat comes 'brown coal', sometimes called 'lignite' or 'cannel coal'. The word 'cannel' is really the same as 'candle'. The name was given to this kind of coal because you could light it with a match and it would burn like a candle. The word 'lignite' means 'like wood'. You can see that this name too is based on the ease with which the coal burns. There is very little of this kind of coal in this country.

Next in the scale of hardness comes bituminous coal. 'Bituminous' means 'tarry'. This is the kind of coal that is used mainly for household fires. It does not light so easily as lignite, but it is not difficult to start it burning because it contains a good deal of tarry matter and gives off gas when heated. It leaves, however, a fair amount of ash.

Next in the scale comes anthracite. This is a very hard coal. It is difficult to start it burning, because it has little tar and gas. It is almost pure carbon. Once it gets going, however, it gives a very hot flame and leaves little ash. It gives hardly any smoke. It is used in stoves for heating water in hot-water systems. It is also used in industry to heat boilers to make steam, for instance in coal-fired power stations.

To sum up, the various kinds of coal are

peat → brown coal → bituminous coal → anthracite
  or
lignite
  or
cannel coal

As we go from peat to anthracite the coal becomes more difficult to burn, the heating value increases, and the amount of ash left behind decreases.

The next experiment shows what happens if coal is heated so that air cannot get to it.

Experiment 12.17
Heating coal

Wear protective goggles while you do this experiment.

Grind up some coal in a mortar. Set up the apparatus shown in Fig. 12.22. Put some of the powdered coal in the tube A. Heat it strongly. Describe the liquid that collects in tube B. Disconnect the apparatus after allowing tube A to cool. Carefully smell the liquid in tube B and test it with indicator paper. While you are heating the coal try to burn any gas given off at C.

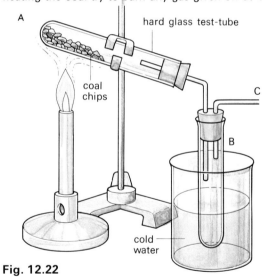

Fig. 12.22

You will have found in this experiment that when coal is heated so that air cannot get to it, a tarry liquid is formed. This is called coal-tar, and a large number of very useful things can be made from it. A gas is also given off, which will burn. This is called coal gas. Until recently it was the gas supplied by the Gas Board. In the home it was used in cooking stoves and gas fires, and for lighting. Now it is either mixed with natural gas, or

natural gas is used by itself for these purposes. So we no longer call the gas supplied to our houses (or to the science room) 'coal gas'.

The solid left behind in the tube after the coal had been heated is coke. In these days coal is very often heated just to get the coke and the coal-tar. The gas is merely a useful by-product. Coke is used as a fuel and in the smelting of metals. It is almost pure carbon. Look back to p. 60 to remind yourself how coke is used in the smelting of iron.

Fig. 12.23 A miner working with a modern coal cutter.

Fig. 12.24 Gas tanks containing liquefied natural gas. Each one holds 20 000 tonnes.

Fig. 12.25 Boys on the Trinidad Pitch Lake showing the consistency of natural asphalt. Find out how this asphalt is removed and exported.

Fig. 12.26 Drilling for oil in a tropical forest.

Fig. 12.27 An oil rig in the North Sea.

12.15 OIL

Another important fuel obtained from the Earth is oil. It has been formed from the decayed remains of sea animals and plants which settled on the floor of ancient seas. As the mud hardened into rocks some of the oily material moved upwards and reached the surface. Here the portions that boil at lower temperatures evaporated away, leaving a tarry deposit. This happened, for example, in the Pitch Lake in Trinidad.

However, most of the oil was trapped by hard rock that it was unable to get through. So in most oil fields it is necessary to drill or bore down through the hard rock to get at the oil below. There is always some natural gas with the oil. If the pressure of the natural gas is high enough it will force the oil up through the bore hole, and it comes gushing out. If there is not enough pressure to do this the oil must be pumped up.

As the oil reaches the surface it does not look very much like the stuff we buy at the garage and use in cars. To make this the oil has to be purified, or refined. The oil coming from the ground is made up of many different substances. These all boil at different temperatures. It is therefore possible to separate them by the process called fractional distillation. You may remember that you used this in Unit 5 to separate alcohol and water.

The portion of the oil (or 'fraction', as it is called) which boils at the lowest temperature contains a good deal of octane. This is used for 'aviation spirit' for aircraft, and high-octane petrol for cars. The ordinary grade of petrol contains less octane and more of the fractions which boil at a slightly higher temperature.

The fraction of the oil which boils at a temperature just above that of the petrol oils is the mixture called 'paraffin oil' (or sometimes 'kerosene'). It is used for burning. The next fraction, with a higher boiling point still, is light lubricating oil – the sort of oil you use in an oil can to oil a sewing machine or bicycle. After this comes the heavier oil which is used to lubricate machinery, such as a car engine. This is the sort of oil poured into the sump of a car. The still higher boiling fractions give vaseline and tar.

The table below shows some of the products obtained in the refining of oil.

Fraction	Uses	Boiling point
'Bottled' gas, Calor gas, or Butane	Compressed and used for heating in portable stoves and cookers, e.g. in caravans	40°C
Petrol	Fuel for internal combustion engines, e.g. cars and planes	40–170°C
Paraffin oil	Burning in stoves; as a fuel for jet engines	150–240°C
Diesel oil	Fuel for some kinds of internal combustion engines, e.g. lorries and buses	220–250°C
Light lubricating oil	Oiling things like locks, hinges, sewing machines, bicycles	250–300°C
Heavy lubricating oil	Oiling heavy machinery, e.g. the bearings of cars and ships' engines	300–350°C
Vaseline, wax, and tar	Lubrication, making roads, etc.	Above 350°C

Of course, not all the crude oil in different parts of the world is exactly the same. It contains different amounts of the fractions mentioned above. Some of it contains a lot of heavy oil, and very little petrol. In order to make more of the fractions with lower boiling points, this heavy oil is **cracked**. This means that it is decomposed into lower boiling oils for which there is a greater demand.

The natural gas which is found in oil fields is mostly made up of methane, a compound of carbon and hydrogen. The discovery of oil deposits below the North Sea, with the natural gas there too, has made it possible to supply most of Britain with this fuel.

Experiment 12.18
Distilling crude oil

Wear safety goggles. You can imitate in the laboratory what is done in an oil refinery. Set up the apparatus shown in Fig. 12.28. Put some crude oil into the test-tube. Heat it gently. Collect the liquid that distils over up to 120 °C. Then change the receiver and collect what comes over up to 170 °C. Change the receiver again and collect further fractions for each 50 °C temperature rise up to 320 °C.

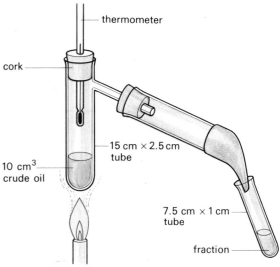

Fig. 12.28

Smell and note the colour of each of the fractions. Find out which of them will burn by pouring some of the liquid into an evaporating dish and putting a lighted taper near it. Put down your results in a table like the one below.

Fraction temperature	Colour	Does it burn? (Yes/No)
Up to 120°C 120–170°C		

12.16 THE SEA

The sea covers a very large area of the surface of the Earth. Any of you who have bathed in the sea will know that sea-water tastes salt. Now you can find out more about this.

Experiment 12.19
Evaporating water

Using a dropper, put three drops of distilled water on a microscope slide. Evaporate them using a very small Bunsen flame, or by shining an infra-red lamp down on the slides. Repeat this with another slide using three drops of tap water, and again with three drops of sea-water. Put the slides on a piece of black paper so that you can see what is left on them. Which kind of water leaves the most solid behind when it is evaporated?

Take a little of the deposit from the sea water on the end of a clean iron wire, or a pencil lead, and hold it in a Bunsen flame. What happens to the flame? Try the same thing with a drop of sodium chloride solution.

Dissolve the rest of the deposit from the sea-water in a few drops of water and add a drop of silver nitrate solution. What happens?

Try the same thing with a drop of sodium chloride solution instead of sea-water.

What do these experiments tell you about the deposit from the evaporated sea-water?

The tests you have just carried out are useful ones for sodium and for a chloride. All sodium compounds give an orange colour to the flame. You may have noticed this when you were boiling some salted water over a gas ring and the liquid boiled over. All solutions containing a chloride give a white colour with a solution of silver nitrate. This colour disappears again when you add some ammonia solution to it. So these experiments tell you, without doubt, that sea-water contains sodium chloride (or common salt).

Sea-water contains many other substances besides sodium chloride. As the shells of animals that live in the sea contain calcium carbonate there must be some calcium compounds in sea-water – otherwise the animals could not make their shells. These compounds are mostly calcium bicarbonate and calcium sulphate. Magnesium chloride and magnesium sulphate are also found in sea-water; at present all the magnesium metal that is made is manufactured from sea-water. Potassium bromide is also there, and most of the bromine that is produced today comes from sea-water.

All salt deposits have been formed by the evaporation of sea-water. So wherever salt deposits are found we may be sure that the area was at one time under the sea. In Britain the largest deposits are in Cheshire. Salt is obtained by pumping water down into them. This forms a large underground lake of salt water. Salt water is called brine. The brine is pumped up and then evaporated. The brine is evaporated in what are called 'vacuum pans' because the pressure of the air above the salt solution is reduced. This makes it possible to evaporate the solution at a lower temperature than normal, and helps to produce the small crystals of salt used in the home.

European salt deposits are also found in Germany, at a place called Stassfurt, and in Poland. Here the salt is mined in the same way as coal, and is not dissolved in water as in Britain.

A large number of very important chemicals are made from salt. That is why Cheshire and South Lancashire form one of the great chemical manufacturing areas of Britain.

12.17 THE CHANGING FACE OF THE EARTH

Most of the land surface of the Earth is covered with a layer of soil. The depth of soil varies from a thin layer about 0.5 cm thick on mountains to a layer two or three metres thick in cultivated areas. How did it get there?

As you read earlier in this Unit (p. 55) rocks are broken down into small particles by the action of the weather. When water freezes it takes up more space. If rain water falls into the cracks between rocks and then freezes, the crack gets bigger, and the rock may split. In some countries there are sheets of ice called glaciers on the mountains. These glaciers gradually slide down the mountain side. As they do so the stones embedded in the ice grind up those on the ground below them into very fine particles. Even the rain very gradually dissolves away some of the rocks it falls on.

Large changes of temperature can crack rocks.

Experiment 12.20
Heating and cooling rocks

Wear safety goggles. Hold a small piece of granite with tongs in a Bunsen flame. When it is very hot drop it into a basin of cold water. What happens?

When the hot granite is dropped into the water it is suddenly cooled. You will find that little bits of the rock break away when it cools. This can happen in nature in very hot places like deserts. The rock gets very hot during the day, but at night it cools down, often quickly.

Other things which can break down rocks are the waves of the sea, and the wind. The sea pounds on rocks with great force and breaks them up. Rivers wear away the rocks through which they pass. Small particles of sand carried by the wind bombard soft rocks and break away parts of them. You may know how uncomfortable it is to walk along the sea shore when a wind is blowing the sand up into your face!

Experiment 12.21
The effect of rivers on rocks

You can imitate the effect of a river on the rocks through which it passes by using a 'stream tray'. This is simply a wooden or plastic tray containing sand. It has an opening at one end, so that water can run away down a sink.

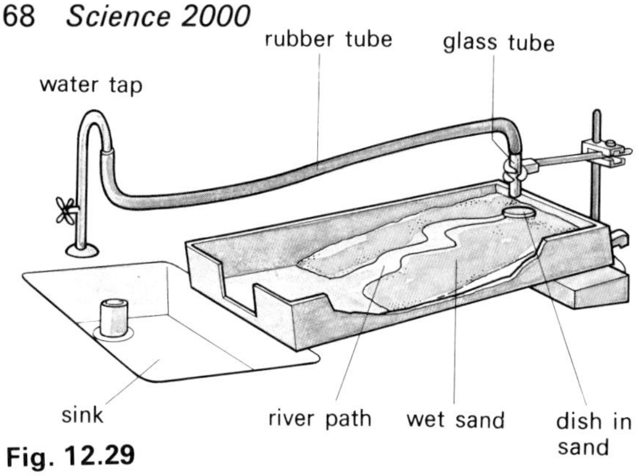

water tap · rubber tube · glass tube

sink · river path · wet sand · dish in sand

Fig. 12.29

First make a wavy path in the sand so that water can run along it. Then let a gentle stream of water run into the tray from a tap for about 15 minutes. Notice what happens to the sand.

You can start again, this time putting a stone in the middle of your river. What effect does this have on the 'banks' of the river?

The little bits of rock which are broken off by weathering either remain on top of the rock or are carried by rivers and glaciers to other places. Small plants grow on top of these rock particles. When they die and decay they form a substance called **humus**, which is dark brown or black. Soil is made up of humus with particles of minerals.

You can find out what is present in a sample of soil. You could spread the sample out on a piece of paper and look at it with a magnifying glass. You could then pick out the plant remains, then the large mineral pieces, then the smaller ones, and so on, but it would take a very long time. There is a quicker way.

Experiment 12.22
Separating soil

Put about 5 cm depth of soil in a jam jar or a measuring cylinder. Fill the vessel about three-quarters full with water, and shake it up. Then set it aside for two or three days.

Now look at the surface of the water. Can you see any remains of plants or humus floating on it? Is the water near the top clear or cloudy? How many layers of soil can you see at the bottom of the jar? Which layer will have the largest particles?

The fine particles 'hanging' or suspended in the water are clay particles. The upper layer of particles which have settled out is probably **silt** or **fine sand**. Below it is a layer of **sand**, and the largest particles at the bottom are **gravel**.

12.18 TYPES OF SOIL

A soil which is made up of very fine particles is called a **clay soil**. The air spaces between the particles are very small, so water cannot pass through them easily and quickly. The soil therefore becomes waterlogged in wet weather and sticks to your shoes. Farmers call this a 'heavy' soil. A soil which is made up of coarse particles is called a **sandy soil**. The air spaces between the particles are large and water can therefore drain through easily. Farmers call a sandy soil a 'light' soil. A mixture of the two kinds of soil is called a **loam**. This is the best kind of soil to have in your garden or on the farm. It neither holds too much water, nor lets it drain away too quickly.

12.19 THE EFFECT OF CULTIVATION ON THE SOIL

Plants require mineral salts, particularly chemicals containing nitrogen, for their growth. They get these substances, dissolved in water, from the soil. They are used to form the stem, leaves, and other parts of the plant. When leaves fall from the plant and rot, and when plants die and decay, these salts are returned to the soil. In this way substances which are necessary for the growth of plants pass from the soil to the plants and back to the soil again.

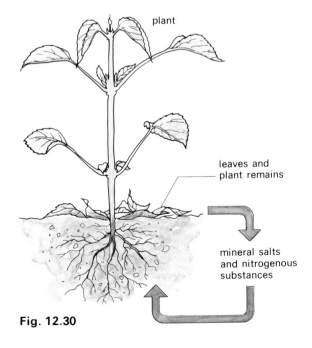

plant

leaves and plant remains

mineral salts and nitrogenous substances

Fig. 12.30

But what happens if plants are removed from the ground and eaten by human beings and other animals? Quite clearly the important chemicals which the plant has taken from the soil are not returned to it. The nitrogen compounds and other chemicals in the plant have been used to build up the animal's body and to give it energy. The excreta of animals contain nitrogen compounds which are very useful to plants. So if animal manure is spread on the ground some of the necessary compounds are returned to the soil.

If the animal dies and its body is returned to the ground, then, as the animal's body decays, these chemicals are once again set free. But in some cases the dead animal's body is not returned to the ground; it may be eaten by other animals, or in the case of humans, it may be burnt up.

So there is a gradual wastage of the chemicals required to keep plants growing healthily. To make up for this the farmer spreads artificial manures, made in chemical factories, on the ground. These are usually called **fertilizers**, because they make the soil more fertile. They simply put back into the soil compounds which the plants need to grow well, and help produce a good crop.

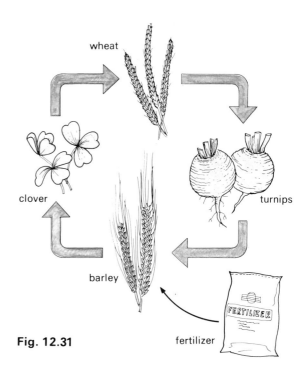

Fig. 12.31

wheat
clover
turnips
barley
fertilizer

12.20 ROTATION OF CROPS

If the same kind of crop is grown year after year in the same field, and the crop is harvested so that nothing is returned to the soil, the essential food chemicals for that crop get used up. In the end the crop gets poorer and poorer.

Cereal crops, like wheat, oats, and barley, use up much of the nitrogen compounds from the soil. On the other hand, bacteria found on the roots of such crops as clover and peas make nitrogen compounds, and put them back into the soil. If clover and peas are grown one year and a cereal crop the next, the nitrogen compounds in the soil should not get used up. So this is what the farmer does. This is called rotation of crops. Figure 12.31 shows a typical four-year rotation.

12.21 CONSERVATION

To make more ground to grow crops on we have, in the past, cleared very large areas of woodland. This happened particularly where settlers had recently arrived. The cleared ground was used mainly for growing only one kind of crop. When the harvests became poor the land was left, and new ground was cleared and planted. The soil left had few plants in it to bind it together, and the top soil was blown away by the wind or washed away by the rain. Large areas of land became **eroded** in this way. Because of people's ignorance, areas that were once fertile have become desert regions.

Today there is a great shortage of food, and we are now trying to turn desert areas back into ground suitable for growing crops.

We are now having to spend a great deal of money to correct mistakes made in the past. Because of the demands for food we must use all the land we can, but we must use the land sensibly and not make it infertile. We must use the land for ourselves; but we must also leave it so that it can still be used for farming many years from now.

This idea of not destroying what we have, but using it in such a way that those who come after us can also benefit from it, is called **conservation**. The word 'conservation' just means 'preserving', or 'keeping as it was'. In the past people have often thought too much of what they could get out of the earth around them, without thinking of future generations, and of how these may suffer for their selfishness. If you read the newspapers you will find that this idea of 'conservation' appears often – just because people are beginning to realize that the stock of things the earth can provide is not endless.

12.22 ANIMALS IN THE SOIL

Have you ever wondered what it would be like to live in the ground? It is dark, cold, and damp. Is it the kind of place you would like to live in? However, it is the home for an enormous number of animals.

Experiment 12.23
Animals in the soil

Dig up a spade-full of soil and put it in a polythene bag. Try to dig fairly deeply and get some damp earth.

In the science room spread out some of the soil you have collected on a sheet of paper and turn it over carefully with a stick to separate the particles. Can you see any animals in it?

Figure 12.32 shows *some* of the animals you might see. If you see any of them in your sample of earth make a list of them. The picture also shows some (such as the snail and the slug) which you might see on the surface of the soil in your garden. If there are animals in your sample which are not in the picture try to find out their names from a book in the library.

Experiment 12.24
Organisms too small to see

Sieve some fresh garden soil.

Look carefully at the sieved soil in the collecting dish. Now use a lens to examine it, or look at some under a microscope. Can you see any living things?

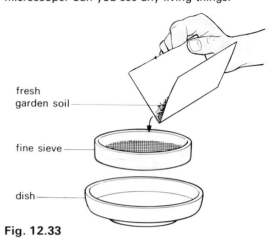

fresh garden soil

fine sieve

dish

Fig. 12.33

Fig. 12.32 Some of the animals you may find in or on the soil.

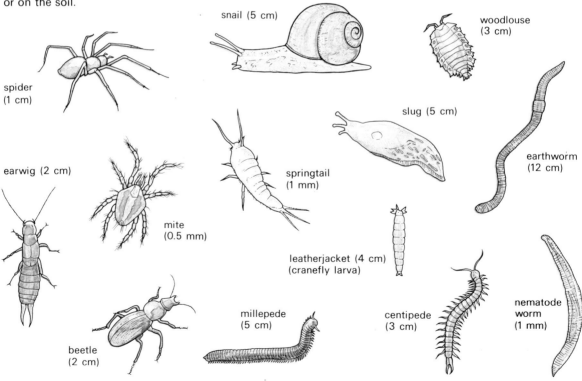

snail (5 cm)

woodlouse (3 cm)

spider (1 cm)

slug (5 cm)

earthworm (12 cm)

earwig (2 cm)

springtail (1 mm)

mite (0.5 mm)

leatherjacket (4 cm) (cranefly larva)

nematode worm (1 mm)

millepede (5 cm)

centipede (3 cm)

beetle (2 cm)

Some organisms are too small to be seen, even with the help of your lens or school microscope. But, the fact that you cannot see them does not mean that they do not exist. These small organisms are called **micro-organisms**. Soil contains many kinds of micro-organisms and you are now going to study some of them. The first kind you are going to deal with are **bacteria**.

12.23 BACTERIA

Although bacteria are too small to be seen, if you grow them, they will increase greatly in number. You will then be able to see, not individual bacteria, but groups or colonies of them. To make them grow you must provide them with food.

12.24 PREPARATION FOR THE GROWTH OF BACTERIA

Your teacher will give you a flat, transparent dish called a **Petri dish** containing a clear jelly. This jelly has food for the bacteria in it. Bacteria are put, or settle onto, the surface of the jelly and use the food to grow. Bacteria occur in many places. In Experiment 12.26 you will try to find some of these places.

In order to grow specific bacteria, you must make sure that there are no bacteria already in the dish or jelly. All the materials and apparatus that you handle will have been **sterilized** before you use them. This means that they have been treated in some way, usually heated for a set time under pressure, to kill any bacteria already in them. Therefore, at the beginning of your experiments, there will be no bacteria in the jelly or the dish.

Experiment 12.25
Soil bacteria

In this experiment you will discover whether your sifted garden soil really does contain bacteria. Your teacher will give you two sterile dishes, A and B, each containing jelly. Shake up a sample of soil in cooled boiled water. Dip a new cotton bud into the soil water and paint one or two lines on the surface of the jelly in dish A. (You could paint your initials.) Quickly replace the lid of the dish. Dip another cotton bud into boiled water alone and draw on the surface of the jelly in dish B. Quickly replace the lid. Seal the lids down with sticky tape and place the dishes in a warm place for a few days. Bacteria grow quickly under warm conditions.

After a few days examine the jelly. **Never remove the lid from the dish**. The creamy coloured circles you see are colonies of bacteria. Draw what you see in each dish.

Note carefully Some bacteria can be harmful to humans and cause disease. As soon as you finish handling the dishes **wash your hands**. Remember, **never** eat anything in the laboratory when you are working with bacteria. Why?

Here are some questions for you to answer about Experiment 12.25.
1 Did your soil contain bacteria?
2 Did the boiled water contain bacteria?
3 Why did you use boiled water, and not water straight from the tap?
4 Why did you set up dish B in this experiment?
Dish B is called a **control**. In this experiment it shows that it was the soil, and not the water mixed with it, which contained the bacteria.

Experiment 12.26
Where else are bacteria found?

Bacteria are found in many places. Let us find some of them. Label six sterile dishes containing jelly A, B, C, D, E, and F. Treat them as follows:
A – paint the surface with some milk.
B – paint the surface with some pond or river water.
C – touch the surface with your finger tips.
D – hold a hamster or mouse (or any other small animal in your laboratory) so that its feet touch the surface of the jelly.
E – leave open to the air.
F – leave unopened.
Seal each dish and leave it in a warm place for a few days. Draw what you see in each dish. Why did you set up dish F?

Experiment 12.27
Bacteria and our food

Set up the apparatus shown in Fig. 12.34 (p. 72) and leave it in a warm place for a few days.

Examine the broth in each tube. What change has occurred in A? What has brought about this change? What has happened in B? Can you explain any difference in the appearance of the broth in the two tubes? What was the purpose of the cotton wool in B? Why were the tubes sterilized as well as the broth?

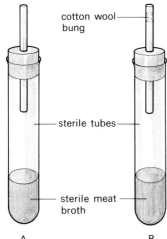

cotton wool bung

sterile tubes

sterile meat broth

Fig. 12.34 A   B

Meat broth is a nutritious food for us, and it also makes a nutritious food for bacteria. Bacteria from the air settle in the broth, feed on it, and rapidly increase in number. The broth soon becomes **contaminated** by the bacteria. If we eat food contaminated by bacteria it can make us very sick. Unfortunately, bacteria seem to like foods that are favourites with us. Cream cakes, meat pies, and meat stews are special favourites. If these foods are kept in a warm place for any length of time they quickly become contaminated, go bad, and must be thrown away. Can you think of two ways to reduce bacterial contamination of cream cakes and pies before you eat them?

12.25 PRESERVATION OF FOOD

Food is too important and too expensive to waste. We must try to keep it fresh for as long as possible. We can help to reduce the number of bacteria settling on our food by keeping it covered. Many methods have been developed for keeping food fresh, and preserving it. Here are some of them – drying, salting, pickling, canning, refrigeration, and deep freezing.

Choose any **two** of these methods and describe how you think they help to prevent food going bad. When you go home, look around the kitchen. Make a list of the methods used to keep food fresh.

Few of the methods of food preservation listed above actually sterilizes food. Under these conditions bacteria are unable to multiply, or do so very slowly, but they are not killed. If something has to be sterilized, say a baby's bottle or food, it can be heated under pressure in a pressure cooker, or a special sterilizing fluid can be used.

12.26 MICRO-ORGANISMS WHICH MAKE US ILL

Contaminated foods are not the only source of harmful bacteria. They are found in soil, in the drains of sinks, in toilets, and in ourselves when we are ill. Micro-organisms which make us ill are usually called **germs**.

You can try to reduce the spread of germs when you are ill by taking sensible precautions. If you have a cold, you should not cough and sneeze into the air. Germs are carried on the tiny droplets of moisture blown into the air from your nose. If you have an illness such as chickenpox or measles you should stay at home in bed, away from your friends, just in case you spread your germs to them.

Fig. 12.35

Something to do at home

At regular intervals throughout your life you have been given injections which help to protect you from certain illnesses.
1 What diseases have you been protected from?
2 What name is given to this method of protection?
3 Find out what you can about Edward Jenner and Jonas Edward Salk.

Experiment 12.28
Other harmful micro-organisms

Your teacher will give you four Petri dishes labelled A, B, C, and D. Cut four pieces of bread to fit the four dishes. Put 100 cm³ of water into a measuring cylinder and carefully add water from the cylinder to the bread in dish A, until the bread is *wet*, but not soaking. How much water did you add to A? Add half of this volume to dish B. Add a quarter of the volume you put into A to dish C. Leave dish D dry. Leave the dishes open for 20 minutes, so that the bread is exposed to the air. Cover each dish and leave them in a warm, dark place for at least a week. Examine each piece of bread and draw what you see.

The felt-like material growing on the bread is in fact a plant. This plant is one of the unusual group of plants called **fungi**. This type of fungus is often called a **mould**.

Fig. 12.36 A mouldy orange.

Estimate the proportion of mould growing on each piece of bread. You can do this as follows. Place your dish on a sheet of graph paper and draw round it. Copy the shape and size of any patches of mould on the bread onto the paper. Count (a) the number of squares covered by the mould and (b) the total number of squares covered by the dish. Suppose the number of squares covered by the mould is 100, and the number of squares covered by the dish is 400. The proportion of bread covered by mould is $\frac{100}{400}$ or $\frac{1}{4}$ or 25%.

Which piece of bread shows the greatest, and which the least growth of mould?

Suggest **two** conditions which are required for the best growth of mould. Where did the mould growing on your bread come from?

Suggest **one** way of preserving foods from moulds.

12.27 USEFUL MICRO-ORGANISMS

You have been looking at micro-organisms which are harmful to humans. Fortunately most micro-organisms are not harmful, and in fact some are very helpful to us.

Experiment 12.29

Take two beakers and label them A and B. Mix four tablespoons of flour and one teaspoon of sugar. Divide the mixture into two. Put one half into beaker A, the other into beaker B. Add 25 cm³ of warm water to A. Add 25 cm³ of warm water and $\frac{1}{2}$ teaspoon of yeast to B. Cover each beaker with a damp paper towel and leave them in a warm place for 30 minutes.

The yeast which you added to B is a fungus.

It feeds on the sugar and produces the gas, carbon dioxide. What function do you think this gas, and so yeast, has in the manufacture of bread?

Home brews If you have ever watched beer or wine being made at home, you will know that yeast and sugar are always added. The yeast reacts with the sugar to make **alcohol**. Carbon dioxide is produced as a waste product, and it is this which forms the froth on top of the fermenting beer or wine. Yeast is a very important fungus indeed.

Some homework for you

Find out the part played by micro-organisms in the making of cheese and yoghurt.

Experiment 12.30

Your teacher will give you a Petri dish in which bacteria have been grown. How can you tell that there are bacteria on the jelly? **Do not touch the surface of the plate, or breathe over it.** Sterilize a pair of forceps in a flame. Allow them to cool, but do not put them on the desk. (Why?) Using the forceps, carefully take a paper disc from the jar, which your teacher will provide, and place it in the centre of the jelly. Cover your dish, label it, and leave it in a warm place for a few days. Examine your dish and in particular look at the area around the disc. What do you see?

impregnated paper disc

Fig. 12.37

The paper disc had been soaked in a broth containing a special fungus. It is said to be **impregnated** with the fungus. The fungus, called *Penicillium*, is very important to humans. It produces a chemical which kills bacteria. In the experiment you should have seen an area of clear jelly around the disc. The fungus produced a chemical which has spread from the disc onto the jelly, where it killed the bacteria which were growing there. The chemical produced by the fungus is called **penicillin**.

If you are ill, you are sometimes given penicillin to take. It kills the bacteria in your body which are making you unwell. Penicillin is one of a group of bacteria-killing substances called **antibiotics**.

Using books in your library, find out about the discovery of penicillin by Sir Alexander Fleming.

12.28 MICRO-ORGANISMS AND YOUR HOME

You now know how important micro-organisms are to us. Some are useful, some are harmful. Your parents spend a great deal of money in order to keep you as free from harmful bacteria as possible, and to preserve your foods.

Write down a list of the products, or the methods used in your home to
1 keep sinks clean;
2 keep drains clean;
3 keep toilets clean;
4 keep cuts clean and reduce infection;
5 prevent cold germs from spreading.

WHAT YOU HAVE LEARNT IN THIS UNIT

1 The Earth has a radius of about 6000 km. It is made up of an outer crust, only a few kilometres thick, then a soft mantle, followed by a liquid core, and then a solid inner core. Figure 12.10 shows this.
2 Some rocks solidified from molten material when the Earth cooled. These are called igneous rocks. They are made up of crystals and contain no fossils.
3 Rocks which have been deposited under water are called sedimentary rocks.
4 Rocks which have been formed from other rocks by the action of heat and pressure are called metamorphic rocks.
5 Not many metallic elements are found as such in nature. This is because metals often combine with oxygen and with sulphur, both of which occur in large quantities.
6 Minerals from which metals are obtained are called **ores**. To obtain the metals the ores are smelted. When ores are heated they are usually changed into oxides. Then the oxygen has to be pulled away from the metal by heating it with a reducing agent, such as carbon, which is used in the form of coke.

7 When most carbonates are heated they give off carbon dioxide and leave the oxide of the metal. Exceptions are sodium and potassium carbonates which cannot be broken down by heating.
8 Coal is the fossilized remains of vegetation. There are various kinds of coal of different ages. They also differ in the ease with which they burn. They are called peat, lignite, bituminous coal, and anthracite. By heating coal so that air cannot get to it, a gas, tar, and coke are obtained. All these products are widely used in industry. Many useful products can be obtained from coal-tar by distilling it.
9 Oil has been produced by the decay of plants and animals. As it comes out of an oil well it is a dark-coloured thick liquid, and is a mixture of various kinds of oil. These are separated by fractional distillation. Crude oil yields petrol, paraffin (or kerosene), lubricating oil, vaseline, wax, and pitch. A great deal of industry is based on oil. It is called the **petrochemical** industry.
10 Sea-water contains many dissolved salts. The most common is sodium chloride (common salt). The sodium chloride used as table salt or in industry is obtained either from the sea itself by evaporation, or from salt deposits. These deposits come from ancient seas which have now dried up.
11 Soil is made up of tiny particles of minerals which have been broken off rocks by the process of weathering, and decayed plant and animal matter called humus.
12 There are three main types of soil: sandy soil, clay soil, and loam (a mixture of clay and sandy soils).
13 The soil provides a home for many animals, and most of the land plants grow in it.
14 Soil contains very small organisms or micro-organisms. Some of these are called bacteria.
15 Bacteria occur nearly everywhere. Some are harmful to us. They contaminate food and make it go bad. Some, which we call germs, make us ill.
16 Most methods of preserving foods do not kill bacteria, but stop them from multiplying.
17 Some micro-organisms are useful to man. Yeast is one, which is used in baking and brewing. Penicillin (extracted from the fungus *Penicillium*) is used to kill certain bacteria in us.

NEW WORDS YOU HAVE MET IN THIS UNIT

alloy a mixture of metals. An example is brass, which is a mixture of copper and zinc.

antibiotic a chemical which kills bacteria.

bacteria single-celled micro-organisms. The singular of this word is bacterium.

clay soil soil made up of very fine particles.

conservation preservation of natural resources from influences which may damage or destroy them.

contaminate infect or pollute.

control part of an experiment set up as a standard which can be compared with other results obtained.

fertilizer a chemical added to the soil to make crops grow better.

fossil the remains of once living things now embedded in rock.

fungus a non-green plant.

germ a micro-organism which makes us ill.

humus part of the soil formed by the decay of plant and animal material.

igneous a rock which has at some time in the past been molten, and has now crystallized.

impregnate to fill or saturate.

loam a well-balanced soil, containing clay, sand, and humus.

metamorphic rock which has been formed from another by the action of heat and pressure.

micro-organism a very small organism, usually made up of only one cell, too small to be seen with the naked eye.

mould a kind of fungus which usually grows on food.

ore a mineral from which a metal is obtained.

penicillin an antibiotic produced by the fungus *Penicillium*.

Petri dish a clear dish used for growing bacteria.

reduction the removal of oxygen from a compound.

sandy soil a soil containing many coarse particles.

sedimentary a rock which has been laid down under water.

sterilize destroy any bacteria.

weathering the effect of the weather – wind, rain, frost – on rocks.

yeast a fungus used in baking and brewing.

SOME QUESTIONS FOR YOU

1 Which of these metals would you expect to find native (that is, not combined with anything else) in the Earth's crust: sodium, gold, zinc, magnesium, silver, platinum, potassium, mercury? Explain your answer.

2 How could you get copper from malachite?

3 Why is jewellery made of silver or gold and not iron or zinc?

4 Explain why loam is a good soil for the growth of most plants.

5 Mention three ways in which you could make a swab of cotton wool sterile.

6 What is meant by the following terms: fractional distillation, smelting, petrochemical industry, conservation?

7 Take a walk around your local supermarket and note how many foods are made with the help of micro-organisms.

Forces and movement

13.1 THE IDEA OF FORCE

In this Unit you are first going to find out something about forces. A force is not something you can see, but is something everyone can give and receive. Through which of your senses do you know about forces? Well, it is through your sense of touch and your sense of sight. You *feel* discomfort or soreness in your muscles when you give a force to anything, and you *see* what forces can do. You may be lifting a heavy object, pushing a lawn mower, pulling a door open, or twisting the cap off a bottle of lemonade. In all these cases you are giving, or **'exerting'** forces. You know this because, if the force you exert is a large one, your muscles get tired. You can also see that sometimes objects are made to move when forces are applied to them. Can you think of other examples of forces?

Fig. 13.1 Exerting force.

Sometimes, no matter how hard you try, you cannot exert a force big enough to move a heavy object. You could not, for example, lift a car by yourself. Make a list of as many inventions as you can which help people to do tasks like this.

From what you have just read you might think that all forces are exerted by people. This is not so. For example, the wind can exert a force and move things; moving water, such as waves, can knock you over; electricity can drive electric motors, and so on.

13.2 SOME EFFECTS OF FORCES

Pushing, pulling, and twisting are all examples of forces you can exert by touching objects with your hands. You are going to find out what happens when you use some of these forces, and you will see the effects for yourselves.

Experiment 13.1
What forces do

The following simple experiments might be arranged so that you can try each in turn.

Fig. 13.3

(a) Pull the elastic luggage holder. What happens to its length?
   Your pull has stretched the luggage holder. What do you notice happening to its thickness?
   Still keeping hold of the hooks, stop pulling. What happens to the holder now?
   A substance is called **elastic** if it returns to its original shape and size when it is not being stretched. Try stretching some Plasticine. Is it elastic?
(b) Make a thick block of Plasticine and place it on the floor. Drop a large steel ball-bearing from the height of the bench onto the Plasticine block, aiming for its centre. What happens to the Plasticine? Does its shape come back when you lift off the ball?
(c) Take a large pad of foam plastic (the sort that is used in seat cushions) and put a large 'weight' on it. What does the force do to the foam pad? We say

Fig. 13.2 Modern lifting gear.

that the pad is **'compressed'**. What happens to the shape of the pad when you take the heavy weight off?

In each of these three simple experiments you saw that the force you used made an object change its shape. The luggage holder was stretched and the cushion pad was compressed. These things were elastic. But the Plasticine did not get its shape back again after it had been compressed, so it is said to be **'inelastic'**.

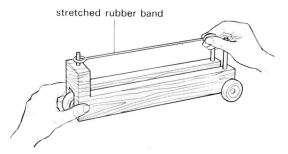

Fig. 13.4

(d) In this experiment you are going to use a smaller elastic band than the luggage holder. It has been specially made for science experiments, and it must not be stretched too much, or it cannot be used again. The band has rings at both ends. Put one ring round the single pin on the trolley as shown in Fig. 13.4. Hold the trolley with one hand at this end, and stretch the elastic until the second ring is exactly over the far end of the trolley, between the two pins.

Now put the trolley on a smooth, clean table. Let go of the trolley, and keeping the elastic band stretched to the same length all the time, pull the trolley along the bench. What happens to the trolley? Do you find that it moves faster and faster as you pull it with the stretched elastic band?

By keeping the elastic stretched to the same amount all the time you are exerting a steady force on the trolley. This steady force caused the trolley to change its speed; at first it was stationary, and then it moved faster and faster as you pulled.

(e) You need a tray containing some tiny polystyrene beads, and some ring magnets (Fig. 13.5).

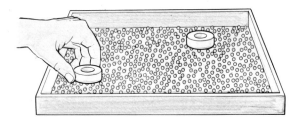

Fig. 13.5

Warning: Do not let any of the beads fall on the floor. Do not drop the ring magnets either. They are sometimes made of a brittle material which chips easily. Try not to allow them to 'click' together, as this breaks tiny chips off them.

Take two of the magnets and find out which way up they have to be in order to **repel** one another. Then put one of them on the beads near one end of the tray. Push the second magnet quite gently

towards the first one from the other end of the tray. What happens when the second magnet approaches the first?

You should find that the beads allow the magnet to glide over the surface of the tray, in much the same way as an ice hockey puck moves over ice.

In this experiment you used a different kind of force than in the other ones – magnetic force. The magnets do not even have to touch to exert a force on each other. This force usually makes the first, stationary magnet change its position, while the second one not only changes its speed, but its direction as well.

To sum up, all these experiments have shown us that forces can change the shape, the speed, and the direction of motion of an object.

13.3 ANOTHER MYSTERIOUS FORCE

You have noticed that the force of magnetism is rather peculiar because it acts from a distance. Two magnetic bodies do not have to touch each other before the force comes into play.

There is another mysterious force rather like magnetism in its behaviour. You will remember that in Unit 7 you rubbed strips of cellulose acetate and polystyrene, and then found that they would attract each other (Experiment 7.2). The force which causes this is an electrical force. Scientists think that electrical forces explain some of the peculiar things about matter.

In your previous work you have built up a picture of what solids are like. For example, in crystals the particles are arranged in ranks and files with spaces between them. But if this is so, what stops the solid from falling to pieces? There must be some kind of force which keeps the particles apart, but at the same time stops them from being pulled apart easily. We believe that this force is an electrical force.

Think about the last experiments you did. In elastic things the forces between the particles must be very strong to bring them back to their old shape after they have been stretched. On the other hand, the forces between the particles in Plasticine cannot be so strong.

13.4 PASSING FORCES ON

When a force is passed on from one thing to another we say it is **transmitted**. Another title for this paragraph would therefore be 'The transmission of forces'.

We are now going to find out which are the best materials for transmitting forces.

Experiment 13.2
Pushing a brick over

(a) Using solids
You will need a wooden rod. Try pushing its ends together. Is it easy to compress? Stand a builder's brick on end on the floor. Try to push the brick over with the wooden rod, first by pushing it near the bottom, then in the middle, and then at the top. Where should you put the rod to push the brick over most easily?

Now get a 'compression spring'. This is a spring which can be pushed in and made shorter in length. When the push is taken off the spring comes out again to its old length. It is the kind of spring used in the shock absorbers of cars and motor cycles. Try to push the brick over with the spring. Which passes on your push to the brick better – the wooden rod or the spring?

(b) Using air and water
First remind yourselves about the compressibility of air and water. Put your finger over the nozzle of a syringe which is full of air. Try to push down the plunger. You will find that you can push it down a little before you have to take your finger off. Now try the same thing with a syringe full of water. In this case you cannot push down the plunger at all. Air, then, is compressible, but water is not.

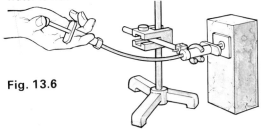

Fig. 13.6

You will need two sets of the apparatus shown in Fig. 13.6. In the one the syringe and tubing are filled with air, and in the other they are filled with water. Put the metal plate attached to the syringe containing air against the brick. Push the plunger in. Can you push the brick over?

Now do the same thing using the syringe filled with water, putting the metal plate in about the same place as before. Can you push the brick over this time?

Remember that the air is compressible and the water is not. This experiment tells us again that forces are transmitted better by materials which are incompressible than by those which are compressible.

13.5 A PRACTICAL CASE: MOTOR CAR BRAKES

Figure 13.7 (a) shows a model of the braking system of a motor car. There are five syringes, and they are connected, as you can see, by T-pieces. One syringe takes the part of the car foot-brake pedal,

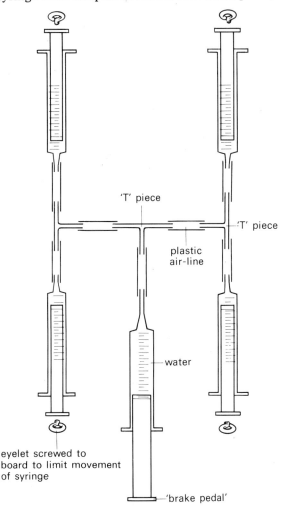

Fig. 13.7 (a)

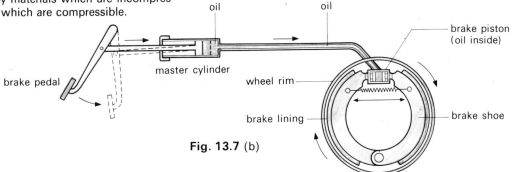

Fig. 13.7 (b)

and the other four represent the brake cylinders for each road wheel. All the syringes are linked, in the model, with plastic tubing, and the system is full of water. When the plunger of the syringe representing the foot brake is pushed in, what happens to the plungers of the other syringes? They should each move out, showing that the force applied to the foot brake is passed onto the brake linings, pressing them against the wheel rims.

In Fig. 13.7(b) this is shown for one wheel only.

Some questions for you to answer

1 Is water used in the hydraulic brake system of a car? If not, what is used instead, and why?
2 If air bubbles get into the tubes of the braking system will the brakes work as well? Why?
3 Brakes with air bubbles in the fluid are called 'soft' – they are obviously dangerous. What do mechanics call the job of removing the air bubbles from the brake fluid?
4 Why do liquids transmit forces well, but gases do not?

An extra experiment

Experiment 13.3
Finding the force needed to pull a door open

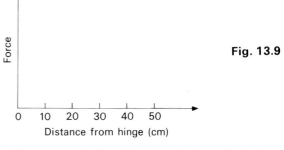

Fig. 13.9

Draw a graph of the force needed to pull the door open plotted against the distance of the force from the hinge (Fig. 13.9). From the graph, what can you say about the force needed as you increase the distance from the hinge?

It is also interesting to make a graph of the force against the reciprocal of the distance (i.e. $\frac{1}{\text{the distance}}$).

Another similar experiment could be carried out on a fire door with an automatic closing mechanism.

13.6 FRICTION

In one of the early experiments in Unit 3 you rubbed your finger backwards and forwards on the bench. In doing this you experienced **friction**, a force which resists and often stops movement. Do you remember where, in bicycles, friction is a useful force, and where also we try to reduce it as much as possible?

Experiment 13.4
Finding out about friction between solids

Fig. 13.8

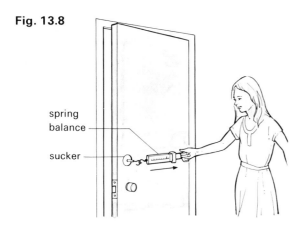

spring balance

sucker

Fix the 'sucker' to the door about 10 cm from the hinge. Tie a spring balance to it as shown in Fig. 13.8, so that you can pull the door horizontally. Take the reading when the door moves steadily towards you. Repeat this at intervals of 10 cm along the breadth of the door. Put down your results in a table.

Fig. 13.10

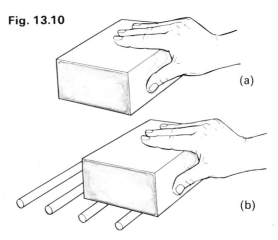

(a)

(b)

You will need a closed box with sand inside. One side of the box is covered with sand paper to make it rough. Another side has a formica surface to make it very smooth.

Place the box with the rough side downwards either on the floor, or on a piece of hardboard on the bench.

Push the box and try to make it slide. Then turn the box over so that the smooth side is downwards and again try to make it slide. On which side does the box slide more easily?

Now try to slide the box on some rollers – round dowelling rod will do. What do you find?

In which case was the effect of friction greatest? In which two ways can friction be reduced?

Experiment 13.5
Experiments with pucks

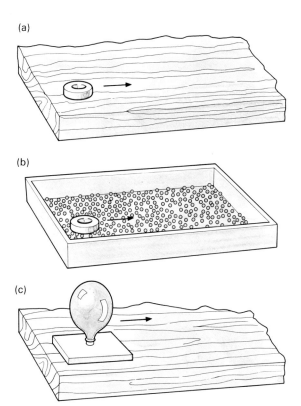

(a)

(b)

(c)

Fig. 13.11

It is best to use a bench with a smooth surface for this experiment. First find whether a brass puck will slide along the top of the bench. Now try gently sliding the same puck over the bottom of a tray, first without and then with polystyrene beads in the tray.

Next blow up a balloon and, holding the neck of the balloon so that the air cannot escape, fix it to the base of a hardboard puck. Put them on the bench, then let go of the balloon and give the puck a gentle push along the bench.

In which case did the puck go furthest? In which was there least friction?

Fig. 13.12 Hovercraft on land and sea. How does it stay afloat and move across the water?

You should have found that the polystyrene beads cut down the friction between the brass puck and the surface of the tray. In the case of the balloon puck there was practically no friction as long as the balloon had air in it, and so it kept going at a steady speed for a long time. What made this happen?

As the air came out of the balloon, it came between the hardboard and bench surfaces and made a kind of cushion of air. So the rough parts of these surfaces did not touch each other. If you have a large balloon try to find out how far your balloon puck can travel over the laboratory floor.

The balloon puck experiment will help you to understand why a hovercraft can travel so fast over land or water. The hovercraft floats on a cushion of air so that there is very little friction between the hull and the surface beneath it (Fig. 13.12).

13.7 FREE-WHEELING ON A BICYCLE

You found that when a puck was pushed on a tray covered with tiny beads there was much less friction than when the puck slid over the tray itself without the beads. We use this idea to reduce the friction in many moving parts of machinery.

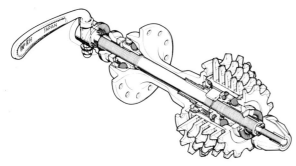

Fig. 13.13 The ball bearings inside a bicycle hub.

Ball bearings are a ring of steel spheres between the moving surfaces. Perhaps you have seen them on parts of a bicycle. The presence of ball bearings makes it possible to 'free-wheel' for a long distance along a flat road before the cycle slows down.

In other kinds of machinery roller bearings are used. You found that rollers could also greatly reduce friction.

Experiment 13.6
Comparing friction in liquids and gases

(a) **Liquids**

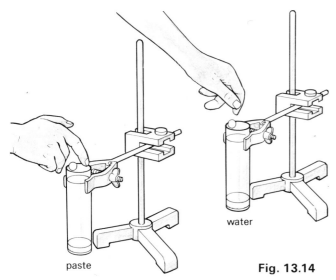

paste   water   **Fig. 13.14**

You need a jar containing wallpaper paste and one containing water. Support them in retort stands and clamps. Take two large ball bearings, one in each hand, and hold them at the rims of the jars. Now drop both the balls into the jars at the same time. In which jar does the ball reach the bottom first?

If you want to check this result and repeat the experiment, hold a powerful magnet against the jar near the ball and draw the magnet slowly up the side of the jar – the ball should follow.

In which liquid is friction greater?

What do you think you would find if you tried this experiment with a jar full of syrup?

(b) **Air**

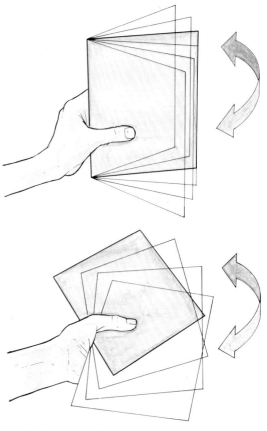

Fig. 13.15

You will need a ceiling tile or a piece of hardboard. First hold the tile straight up and down and wave it from side to side. Then hold it out flat and again wave it from side to side as shown in the diagram. Which way is it easier? Can you explain why?

Here is a rather similar experiment. Hold a sheet of paper at arm's length straight out in front of you. Let it fall. Why, do you think, does the paper not fall straight down? Now pick up the sheet of paper and crumple it into a ball. Hold it at arm's length and let it fall again. What happens this time? Why is there any difference?

(c) **Comparing water and air**
Make two balls of Plasticine of the same size as the steel ball bearing you used in part (a) of this experiment. You will also need two jars, one containing water and the

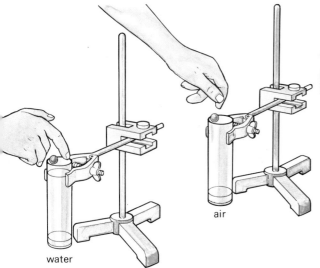

air

water

Fig. 13.16

13.9 MORE EXAMPLES OF FRICTION

Experiment 13.7
Finding the best shape for rapid motion

Fig. 13.17

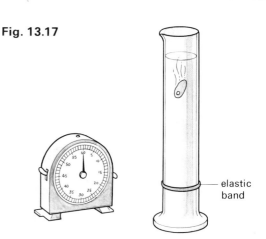

elastic
band

other only air. As you did before, drop one of the Plasticine balls into each of the jars at the same time. Which ball reaches the bottom of the jar first? Can you explain why?

This experiment shows us that friction is much greater in liquids than in gases.

Using our model of the nature of solids, liquids, and gases, can you explain why this should be? Can you think of anything that might give even less friction than a gas?

13.8 FREE-WHEELING IN SPACE

Beyond a height of about 200 miles above the Earth there is so little air that it cannot be detected. If there is no air, there can be no friction and so something moving in space cannot be slowed down by this force. About 300 years ago Sir Isaac Newton predicted that if an object was taken up to a height of 200 miles and then fired horizontally at 28 000 km per hour (18 000 miles an hour) it would continue in orbit round the Earth. Once at this speed it would not need any more force to keep it going, and it would 'free-wheel' in space.

As you know, this prediction has been found to be true. There are now many space satellites which have been orbiting the Earth for many years. They do not slow down because there is no friction to oppose their motion. However, when the satellite is made to come back to Earth it has to pass through the Earth's atmosphere, and the friction between it and the air makes it get so hot that it can be completely burnt up.

You need a tall jar or a measuring cylinder containing wallpaper paste. Put an elastic band round the jar and slide it down to about 4 cm from the bottom. Now take a block of Plasticene and cut pieces from it. These should all have the same weight, say 15 g, and you should test this on a balance. Make each piece into a different shape. You are going to drop them into the jar of paste. Push a 3 mm ball bearing into the front part of the shape so that each piece will travel front end first.

Place all your shapes on a piece of paper and trace round the outside of each one with a pencil. Now drop one of the shapes into the jar of paste and at the same time start a stop clock. Stop the clock when the front end of the shape arrives at the finishing line marked by the elastic band.

Repeat this for the other shapes, writing down the time you recorded inside the tracing of that shape.

Did all the shapes take the same time to fall through the same distance? If not, why do you think there was any difference?

You probably found that the fastest shape was the one that was **streamlined** – like the body of a fish or an aircraft. Streamlining reduces friction. Streamlined objects can move faster through liquids and gases than non-streamlined ones, even though the same pushing or pulling force is applied to them.

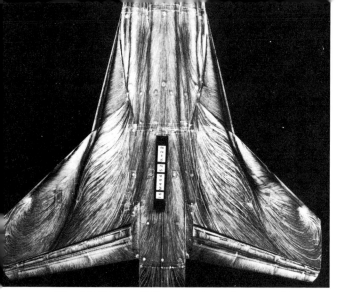

Fig. 13.18 An oil film can show the streamlines on a model of an aircraft.

13.10 FRICTION AND HEAT

You have already found that when you rubbed your finger over the rough surface of the bench your finger got hot. This was due to the fact that you had to supply much more movement energy than if you pushed your finger over a smooth surface. This extra movement energy required to overcome friction was changed into heat.

Look at your finger tip with a magnifying lens. You will see that it has quite a rough surface with the skin raised into ridges. If you look at the bench top with a magnifying lens you will find that it also looks quite rough. When you rub your finger over the bench these rough bits tend to lock into each other. This is how the opposing force of friction arises.

Experiment 13.8
Overcoming friction and changing move-ment energy into heat

Fix a metal rod into a vice. Take a hacksaw and feel the temperature of the blade by touching it with a finger-tip. Now use the hacksaw to cut a slot in the metal rod. When you have cut about half way through stop sawing, and feel the part of the blade that has been doing the cutting. What do you feel?

The teeth of the blade are very rough and jagged, and a lot of the movement energy you have put in has been used to overcome friction and has been changed into heat.

The energy you supplied has also been changed into other forms. Can you say what these are?

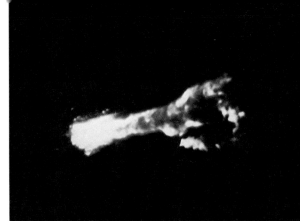

Fig. 13.19 The Appollo command module shown here had a special shield which burned in a controlled way and used up the heat produced on re-entry. This protected the astronauts inside the module.

In Section 13.8, about free-wheeling in space, it was said that a space satellite returning to Earth would pass through the Earth's atmosphere, and that the friction between the satellite and the air would produce a great amount of heat, enough to burn it up. This would not matter if it was not necessary to recover the instruments in the satellite or if the satellite was unmanned. If, however, there were astronauts on board and the spaceship was brought back to Earth, it would have to be specially protected. This is done with a heat shield.

Here again the energy that is used in overcoming friction is changed into heat and other forms. What other forms?

What happens to meteors as they enter our atmosphere from space?

Experiment 13.9
Reducing friction

First try pushing a metal rod into the hole of a rubber stopper. Is this easy to do? What is opposing your force? Remove the rod from the stopper and wet it with water. Try to push the rod into the stopper now. Is it as difficult as before?

Friction is generally not so great when the rubber is wet. If you were wearing rubber-soled shoes would you slip more easily on a dry or a wet floor? Would a motor car skid more easily on a dry or a wet road?

Fig. 13.20

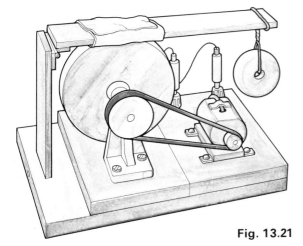

Fig. 13.21

For the next experiment you need the apparatus shown in Fig. 13.21, which consists of some pieces from an energy conversion kit. First wrap a strip of dry brake-pad material round the horizontal brake arm, so that the weight at the end of the arm pulls the pad onto the flywheel. Now raise the brake arm and switch on the power pack connected to the electric motor. When the motor is driving the flywheel at its top speed, switch off the motor and lower the brake arm so that the brake pad rubs against the flywheel. As soon as the brake pad touches the wheel, switch on a stop clock and measure the time it takes for the wheel to stop after the brake has been supplied.

Next remove the strip of brake-pad material and replace it with a piece that has been oiled. Repeat the experiment to find the time it takes to stop the flywheel spinning using the oiled brake-pad material.

Wipe any oil off the flywheel with a clean rag.

Has the oil on the brake pad had any effect on the friction?

Oil is used in machinery to reduce the friction between moving parts. It is often called a **lubricant**.

An extra experiment

Experiment 13.10
Which surface gives a model car better grip?

The equipment needed is shown in Fig. 13.22. The ramp you are using has a formica surface. The slope is adjustable. Wind up the toy car and set it to climb up the

Fig. 13.22

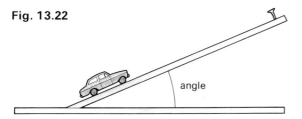

angle

ramp. Alter the angle of the ramp until the wheels just start to slip and the car will not climb the slope. Measure the angle of the slope with a protractor.

Hang a sheet of some other material over the ramp by using the nail at the top of the slope. Repeat the experiment and again find the angle at which the car wheels just start to slip. Repeat the process for as many different surfaces as you can.

Make a table of your results showing the angles you read for the different surfaces. Which surface gave the best grip?

13.11 MEASURING FORCES

In many experiments it is important to be able to measure accurately the size of a force. One way of doing this is by using a spring balance. The next experiment shows you how this works.

Experiment 13.11
The spring balance

(a) **Pulling on an elastic rope with a horizontal force**

This experiment is similar to Experiment 13.1(a). Hold one end of the rope in each hand and pull horizontally. What happens to the length of the rope? Now pull harder until you are pulling as hard as you can. What happens to the length of the rope as you pull harder?

The harder you pull the longer the rope gets. The rope is said to **extend**. Of course, if the elastic was not very strong you might, by pulling hard, be able to break it.

(b) **Pulling on a spring with a downward force**

Set up a spring so that it hangs from a clamp on a retort stand, as shown in Fig. 13.23. Fix an arrow made of

Fig. 13.23

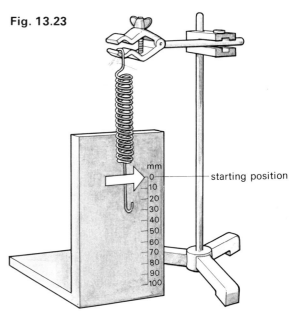

starting position

cardboard to the bottom end of the spring so that you can mark its position on a paper scale pinned to a wooden stand or a box. Mark the position of the arrow with a clear horizontal line. This is the starting point from which you will be making measurements.

You will use various sets of objects as weights and hang them from the hook at the end of the spring. Thus, you might have a set of slotted weights which come with a carrier to hang them by, or you might have a set of washers, or cotton reels. The important thing is that all the objects in your set must be the same in size.

Hang one of the objects on the spring. The spring will stretch. Make sure that the spring and the object on it are hanging freely and not scraping against the scale behind them. Mark the position of the arrow on the scale, and put the number 1 against it. Measure the distance of the mark from the starting point. Note this down in a table of results like the one below.

Number of objects	Increase in length

Put another of the objects onto the spring, and mark where the arrow comes to now. Do this for three and then for four objects on the spring. Make a graph from your table of results, plotting the increase in length (extension) vertically against the number of objects horizontally.

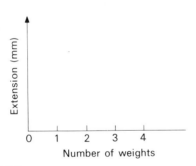

Fig. 13.24

From your graph, predict the increase you would get in the length of the spring if you hung 5 objects on it. Then test your prediction experimentally.

Objects are pulled towards the Earth by the force of gravity. Because all the objects you used in this experiment were identical they were each pulled to the Earth by the same force. This force is called the **weight** of the object. The weight of an object is thus the force that is exerted on it by the Earth. You have just made a simple balance

for measuring the pull of the Earth on things. It is called a **spring balance**. Suppose cotton reels were the objects you hung on your spring. Your graph could be used to find the pull of the Earth on any other object in terms of the pull on a cotton reel. Just hang the object on the spring and find how much the spring stretched. Try this out by hanging some different objects on your spring.

13.12 THE UNIT OF FORCE – THE NEWTON

You and your classmates may all have used quite different sets of objects in making the scales for your spring balances. This would be very inconvenient in practice, because everybody would be using a different unit for measuring forces. It is easier to decide on one particular unit of force which everybody will use. The unit of force which is used throughout the world is called the **newton**. A newton is about the weight of a medium-sized apple. The unit is named after the great scientist Sir Isaac Newton, who lived from 1642 to 1727. He is famed for his work on the study of gravity. Find out all you can about him from a book in the library.

Fig. 13.25 Sir Isaac Newton.

Experiment 13.12
The newton spring balance

This is a spring balance with a scale marked off in newtons. You know that the weight of a body is the force of gravity on it, so the weight of anything, as it is a force, should be measured in newtons.

Object	Weight in newtons

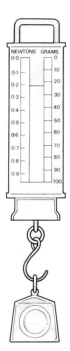

Fig. 13.26

Find the weights of any objects you wish by hanging them on the hook of the spring balance. Record your results in a table like the one shown above. If you have blocks of metal marked 100 g and 1 kg, find their weights in newtons also. You should find that the weight of 100 g (0.1 kg) is about 1 newton. This is written 1 N. The weight of a mass of 1 kg is about 10 N.

Would the results be the same on another planet where the force of gravity is different from the gravity on Earth?

13.13 MASS AND WEIGHT

The mass of a body is the quantity of matter or stuff in it, whereas the weight of a body is the pull of the Earth on it. The weight of anything depends on the amount of stuff in it. To make this clear you have just found that the pull of the Earth on (or the weight of) two cotton reels is twice as big as the pull on one. As the reels are the same size there will be twice as much stuff in two reels as there is in one. So the weight of any object is connected in a simple way with the amount of stuff in it (or its mass). Double the mass and you double the weight; three times the mass, three times the weight, and so on. But remember that although mass and weight are simply connected they are not the same thing.

It is easy to become confused between mass and weight because very often people who are not scientists, and sometimes even those who are, use the same units for mass as they do for weight. Mass is measured in grams or kilograms, and weight in newtons, yet very often you will find people saying that the weight of something is 'so many grams'. This has become so common that we just have to accept it. However, you must keep your wits about you, and remember what people are talking about when they express weight in the wrong units!

The amount of matter or stuff in anything is always the same, no matter where it is. Thus, whether it is on the Earth or on the Moon a particular apple might have a mass of 100 g (0.1 kg). Its weight on Earth would be about 1 newton. But its weight on the Moon would be very different because the force of gravity on the Moon is only about one-sixth of the force on Earth. The apple would therefore weigh only about one-sixth of a newton on the Moon.

It is interesting to work out what would happen if you 'weighed' an apple on the Moon with a double pan balance and with a spring balance. With a double pan balance you put the apple on one pan and 'weights' on the other. You would go on adding weights until the scales 'balanced'. The force of gravity affects both the weights and the apple in the same way. The force of gravity on the apple is only one-sixth of what it was on Earth, but it is also only one-sixth as large on the weights. So, the apple would appear to weigh the same on the Moon as it does on the Earth. However, if you used a spring balance you would be measuring the pull of the Moon on the apple directly; you would not be comparing it with the pull of the Moon on a set of weights. So on a spring balance the apple weighs less on the Moon than it does on Earth – although it is the same apple!

In the same way as you can tell the size of a force from the amount it extends a spring, you can measure a force by the amount it compresses a spring.

Bathroom scales are a type of compression balance. Stand on the scales and find your weight. You will probably find that the scale is marked off in kg and g. If the reading is 40 kg your mass is 40 kilograms, and your weight, the force of gravity on you, is about 400 N.

Use these scales to find how hard you can push, how hard you can grip, and how hard you can hug. Make sure you change your results from the units on the bathroom scales into the correct unit of force, the newton.

13.14 THE LEVER

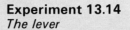

knitting   elastic
needle   band

Fig. 13.28

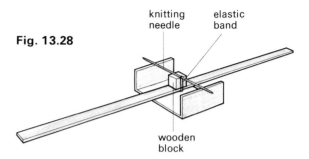

wooden
block

The components shown in the diagram should first be assembled so that the stick is balanced at its centre. If one end is pushed down gently, then the stick should swing back into its position of balance.

(a) Where to push to lift a heavy load
Put a metal weight at the end of one arm of the stick. Push downwards on the other arm of the stick with one finger at different places along the stick. Where is it easiest to push and so balance the load? You should find that the load is most easily balanced when you push at the end as far from the balancing point (the **pivot**) as possible.

A stick used in this way is called a **lever**.

(b) Balancing two counters by using one counter
Put two counters two spaces from the pivot. The line marking this distance must pass through the centre of the counters. Now put one counter on the other arm and move it about until it balances the other two. How far from the pivot must it be placed?

You will find that a single counter can balance two similar counters if it is twice as far out from the pivot.

(c) Take a large number of your counters and pile them on top of one other. Stand the pile on the stick and see if you can balance it with a much smaller pile. Notice where you have to place the counters.

You should find that the large number of counters have to be placed near the pivot, while the smaller number have to be placed on the other arm at a much greater distance from the pivot.

(d) Balancing two counters with another two
Place two counters 5 spaces from the pivot. Find where on the other arm two counters have to be placed to balance the lever.

(e) Balancing three counters with two others
As each counter is pulled equally by the Earth's force

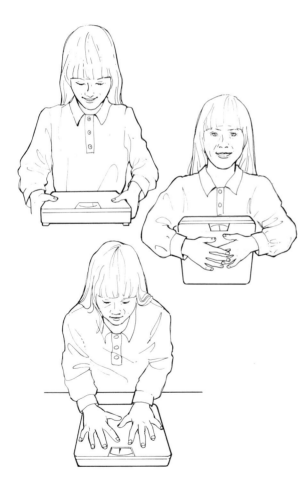

Fig. 13.27

of gravity, you can now say that each counter represents one unit of force. Apply three units of force four spaces from the pivot and find where on the other arm two units of force will balance them.

(f) Further experiments

Try several other arrangements of forces, one on each arm, seeing if you can predict the size of force and distance from the pivot you will need to balance the lever. Check your prediction by experiment.

Perhaps, when making your predictions, you used a rule that you have discovered. What is this rule?

You have found out the following things:

1 The ability of a force to turn a lever about a pivot depends on the distance from the pivot at which the force is applied. The greater the distance from the pivot the greater is the turning effect of the force.

2 The greater the force the greater is its turning effect.

Indeed, you can work out the **turning effect** of a force by multiplying the size of the force by its distance from the pivot.

3 When a lever is balanced the turning effects on both sides of the pivot are the same.

This is called the lever rule – you probably found it out for yourself, and used it in your predictions in experiment (f) above.

Experiment 13.15
The see-saw

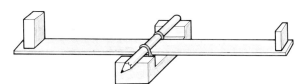

Fig. 13.29

Figure 13.29 shows a model see-saw with a large block of wood on one end and a smaller block of wood on the other. These blocks represent a fat and a thin pupil! Does the see-saw balance? Which 'pupil' turns the see-saw more? What change would have to be made to the positions of the 'pupils' to balance the see-saw? Try it to see if you are right.

You would have to move the fat 'pupil' towards the pivot. However, if both 'pupils' are kept right at the ends there is another way of balancing the see-saw. It is to change the position of the pivot.

Which way should you move it? Well, you have to reduce the turning effect of the fat 'pupil' and increase that of the thin 'pupil'. Using the lever rule you can see that you could do this by moving the position of the pivot towards the fat 'pupil'. Try and see if this works.

Here again you see that by using a lever you can make a small force balance, or even overcome, a much larger force if the small force is far enough away from the pivot.

13.15 LEVERS IN EVERYDAY LIFE

Can you identify where the pivot is and where the best place to apply the force (called the effort) is in these pictures of 'levers'?

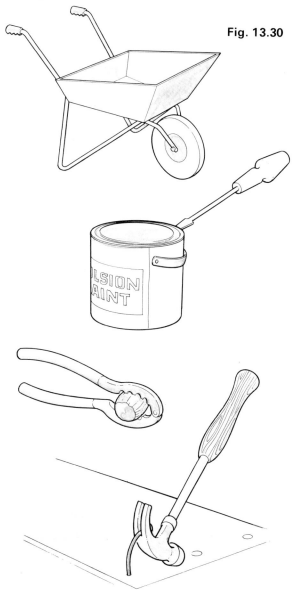

Fig. 13.30

13.16 SOME PROBLEMS TO WORK OUT

Use the lever rule to find the answers to these problems.

1   A crow-bar is used to tilt a block of stone of mass 500 kg. If the lever is pivoted 20 cm from the stone, how far along the bar on the other side of the pivot would a man of mass 100 kg have to stand so that he just lifts the stone?

2   A super-heavyweight wrestler of mass 180 kg sits on a see-saw 50 cm from the pivot. Find your own mass in kg and work out how far away from the pivot on the other arm of the see-saw you would have to be to balance him.

13.17 AN EXTRA EXPERIMENT

Experiment 13.16
A sensitive balance to weigh tiny objects (a straw balance)

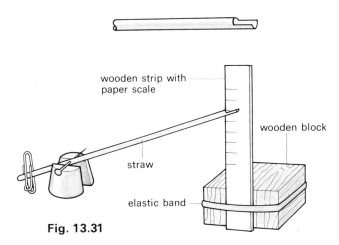

wooden strip with paper scale

wooden block

straw

elastic band

Fig. 13.31

First shape the end of the drinking straw as shown in Fig. 13.31. This makes a little platform on which the tiny objects to be weighed will be placed. Fit the paper-clip into the other end of the straw. This will act as a counterbalance. Try balancing the straw on your finger to find where the centre of balance is. Push a pin or a needle through the upper part of the straw at this point. Balance the straw as shown, adjusting the clip until the straw is pointing to the top of the paper scale. Make sure that the clip does not touch the bench.

You now have to calibrate the scale. Ordinary weights are, of course, much too big for this balance. To make suitable weights get a big sheet of squared paper and weigh it. Suppose its mass is 1 g. Work out the number of squares on the sheet. Suppose there are 1 000. Then the mass of each square is a thousandth of a gram, or 0.001 g. Your sheet may not work out so easily as this, for we have chosen very simple numbers as an example. If you use the same method you will be able to find out what one square of your paper weighs.

Take enough of your squares to have a mass of 0.01 g, place them on the platform of the straw and mark the place where the platform points to. Place another 0.01 g on the platform, and make a second mark on the scale. In this way calibrate the whole scale.

You can now use this balance to weigh a hair, a sugar crystal, a dead fly's wing, and so on.

13.18 MACHINES FOR LIFTING THINGS

A crow-bar is a lever which is often used for lifting heavy loads using a small force. The load will be moved through a very small distance, but, because the effort is applied as far from the pivot as possible, the effort has to move through a much greater distance.

Experiment 13.17
The block and tackle

girder

block and tackle

strong sling

Fig. 13.32

The arrangement of pulley wheels shown in the diagram is called a block and tackle. It can be used, for instance, to lift heavy objects like motor car engines, and to adjust yacht sails. There will probably be a block and tackle fixed up in one of your technical department rooms.

Find the weight in newtons of a pupil who is willing to be lifted. Attach a suitable newton spring balance to the end of the rope so that by pulling on this balance you can find the force required to lift him or her a few centimetres off the floor. Measure the distance the pupil is lifted and the distance the spring balance has to be pulled at the same time. What do you find about the effort force compared with the weight lifted? How does the distance your effort force moved compare with the distance you moved the load?

Experiment 13.18
Pairs of forces

1   Take a dynamics cart, or trolley, as it is called for short. Compress the spring, and put the trolley by itself on the bench. Trigger off the spring. Does the trolley move?

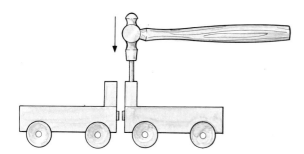

Fig. 13.33

2   Now compress the spring again, place the trolley end to end with another trolley, and trigger the spring. What happens this time?
    You should find that the single trolley does not move as it does not have anything to push against. Repeat the experiment with the single trolley, but this time put the palm of your hand against the compressed spring. Trigger off the spring. What happens this time? You should have felt the spring push against you while the trolley then recoiled backwards.
    From this you can see that forces must occur in pairs. The two trolleys could be said to have exploded – the spring of the first trolley pushed the second trolley away and the first trolley recoiled as a result.

Fig. 13.34

3   You and your partner should put on roller skates – do **not** use trolleys. Stand facing each other and both push at the same time. Who moves? If only one of you does the pushing, who moves?

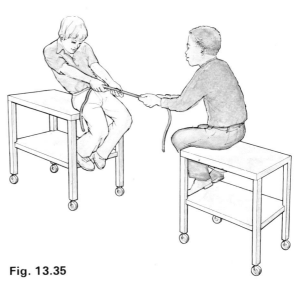

Fig. 13.35

4   This time you should each sit on a science department trolley 2 to 3 m apart. Each hold an end of a piece of stout cord. What happens when you both pull the cord? What happens when only one of you does the pulling?

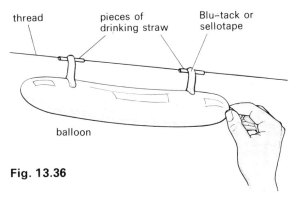

thread | pieces of drinking straw | Blu–tack or sellotape

balloon

Fig. 13.36

5 Blow up a long thin balloon and hold the neck tightly so that the air cannot escape. What happens when you release the balloon? You can also do this experiment by attaching the balloon to a drinking straw and threading it onto thin string stretched across the room (see Fig. 13.36).

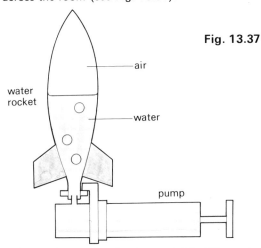

Fig. 13.37

air

water rocket

water

pump

6 This experiment must be done outside. Fill a water rocket half full of water and then pump in some air with about twenty strokes of the pump. Now release the rocket. What happens?

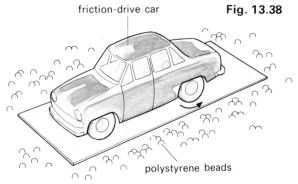

friction-drive car   **Fig. 13.38**

polystyrene beads

7 Scatter a thin layer of polystyrene beads on a large tray and cover these with a sheet of paper. Now wind up a toy car. Put the car with its wheels spinning on top of the paper. What happens?

In part 3 of this experiment, your partner was not the only one to move when you pushed, you moved also.

Part 4 showed you that two forces must have been acting here too. You pulled your partner, and because of this your partner was pulling on you too, although he or she might not have been intending to do so.

In part 5, when the neck of the balloon was released, the air was forced out in one direction while the balloon was pushed in the opposite direction. Similarly, in part 6, the water rushed out from the rocket in one direction and the rocket took off in the opposite direction.

These experiments tell you a little about how space rockets, fireworks rockets, and jet engines work.

13.19 WORK AND ENERGY

In Unit 3 you found out a great many important facts about energy. Energy, like forces, is invisible. Do you remember that we convert the chemical energy in the food we eat into mechanical energy? Using this energy we can do quite hard physical work.

Experiment 13.19

(a) **Lifting different amounts of sand**

Fig. 13.39

You have three plastic sacks, each filled with a different amount of sand. Call these amounts 'small', 'medium', and 'large'.

Lift each sack in turn from the floor onto the bench. Which sack needs the biggest force to lift it? In which case did you do most work? Which sack made you use up most energy?

You have used up some of the chemical energy in your food to carry out the task. What is the energy in the sacks called now that they have been lifted up onto the bench? Touch your forehead. What do you feel? Does this suggest another kind of energy you have made? You had to do most work with the sack which needed most force to lift it.

(b) Lifting the same amount of sand to different heights

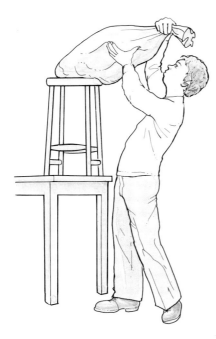

Fig. 13.40

Use the 'medium' sack. This time try lifting it, starting from the floor each time, onto a stool, then onto the bench, and then onto a stool on top of the bench.

In which of these three exercises did you do most work? In which position did the sack have most energy? What kind of energy had the sack been given? From the evidence of your forehead, what other kind of energy have you made?

You had to do the most work when you lifted the sack up through the greatest vertical distance. You can see that the work you do increases as the force you use increases, and as the distance you move the object increases. The amount of work done is measured using the rule:

work done = force × distance moved by the force

(c) Dragging a sack different distances

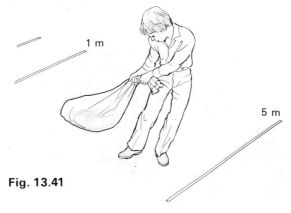

Fig. 13.41

Take the 'large' sack and place it on a trolley. You are going to drag this sack over different distances along the corridor, the entrance hall, or the playground. Chalk a starting line on the ground and mark lines 1 metre, 5 metres, and 20 metres from it. Write the distance at the end of the line. Ask your partner to wheel the sack to the starting line and take it off the trolley for you. Now drag the sack over the 1 metre distance. Ask your partner to lift the sack back onto the trolley and take it to the start again. This time drag the sack for 5 metres; then start again and drag it for 20 metres. Each time your partner must return the sack to the line for you.

Over which distance did you do most work? What force did you have to pull against this time?

In experiments (a) and (b) you lifted the sacks up and the sacks gained potential energy. What has happened to the energy you supplied in experiment (c)?

13.20 OUR BODY AS AN ENGINE

Start by thinking about a motor car. A car is supplied with petrol which is a form of chemical energy. Inside the car engine the petrol vapour is mixed with air. It then burns very quickly, or, as we say, it explodes. What kind of energy does this burning produce? As you would imagine, much heat is produced. Part of this heat is changed into movement energy to drive the working parts, and to overcome the friction opposing their movement. At the same time much heat goes to waste. This wasted heat has to be dispersed, or else the engine would become too hot; the moving parts would expand and the engine would seize up.

Look back to Unit 9 to remind yourself of the ways in which heat can travel. Then find out for yourself how waste heat in a car engine is got rid of, and how the engine is cooled.

In some ways our bodies are similar to engines. Our fuel is the food we eat and we 'burn' this in our bodies to release energy so that our muscles can do work for us. When we do this work we change energy from one form to another, but, as in the car engine, some energy is lost as heat. While you were doing the lifting and dragging experiments you certainly became hot. How do you get rid of this waste heat? When you touched your forehead you probably found traces of sweat. When this sweat evaporates it carries off heat and thus helps you cool down.

13.21 BONES, BONES

In Experiments 13.19 (a) and (b) you lifted sacks from the floor onto benches, and in (c) you dragged sacks along the ground. What parts of your body did you use to do this work? If you do some exercises that you have not done for a long time, which parts of your body ache afterwards?

The answer to both these questions is 'your **muscles**'. You use your muscles to move parts of your body. But could you move as you do, work as you do, and exercise as you do, if you had no bones? Suppose you were just a mass of jelly, like a jellyfish, do you think you would then be able to lift and pull sacks as well as you can now? Do you think you could even stand up without your bones inside you?

Your bones form a part of your body called the **skeleton**.

13.22 THE SKELETON

You are held up, or supported, by your skeleton, which is inside you. Look at Fig. 13.42 or a model of the human skeleton.

Find the backbone, or spine. This is the central support of the body. Does it contain one long bone or many small ones? Run your finger down your own spine or a friend's spine. What are the small lumps you can feel? Your skeleton is made up of a large number of bones. Some are small, like those in the backbone. Look carefully again at the skeleton. Where else can you see very small bones?

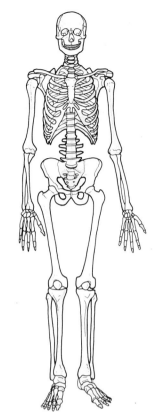

Fig. 13.42

A human skeleton.

Fig. 13.43 (a) The skeleton of a horse.
13.43 (b) The skeleton of a whale.

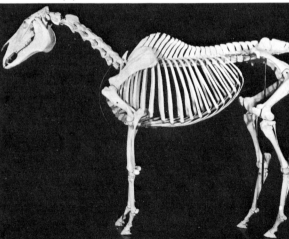

Fig. 13.44 Do these animals have hard external skeletons?

Other bones are long, like those in the arms and in the legs. Now look for the rib cage. What shape is it? What organs of the body would you expect to find inside it? What is the function of the rib cage? Look at the skull. Is it made up of one bone or many bones? What is found inside your skull?

Your skeleton has three main functions. It supports your body. It protects important organs inside you, such as your brain, heart, and lungs. It allows you to move.

In Unit 2 you looked at animals with backbones inside them.

Such animals are called **vertebrates**. However, the majority of animals do not have backbones inside them. These are the **invertebrates**. How do you think these animals support their bodies?

Figure 13.44 shows you some invertebrates. These animals have firm or very hard skins which act as skeletons. Their skeletons are outside their bodies.

13.23 SUPPORT IN PLANTS

Animals are not the only living things that need support. Plants must be supported too. The following photographs show you three ways in which plants are supported.

Figure 13.45 shows seaweed in water. If seaweed is washed up onto the beach, does it remain upright?

Figure 13.46 shows a house plant. If you forget to water plants, what happens to them? Do they remain upright?

Figure 13.47 shows a large tree. What is round the tree? Is the centre of a large tree hard or soft?

Water supports certain plants. Some live in water and are held upright by it. Young seedlings are held up by the water inside them. If you forget to water them, they lose water, wilt, and collapse. Trees have strong bark around them and strong woody tissue inside. Both of these give support to the trees.

13.24 MUSCLES

Look again at the human skeleton (Fig. 13.42). Examine an arm and find out where the arm can bend. You should see three places where bending can take place, at your shoulder, at your elbow, and at your wrist. There is a joint in each of these regions.

Experiment 13.20

Stretch out your arm. Grip the upper part of your arm with your other hand. Slowly bend your upstretched arm from the elbow. Which part of the upper arm gets thicker? Can you explain why?

Experiment 13.21

Your teacher will show you a model of your arm, like the one in Figure 13.48. Look for the bones. What are attached to them?

Figure 13.49 shows the bones of the arm and the muscles attached to them. It is the muscles that move the bones in the body. Name the structures which attach the muscles to the bones.

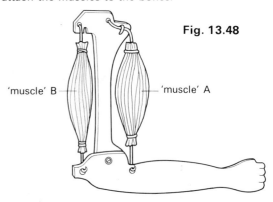

Fig. 13.48

'muscle' B

'muscle' A

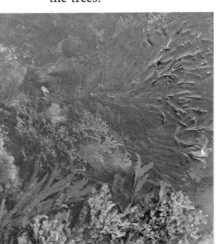

Fig. 13.45 (left) Seaweed.

Fig. 13.46 (below) A non-woody pot plant.

Fig. 13.47 (right) A mature tree.

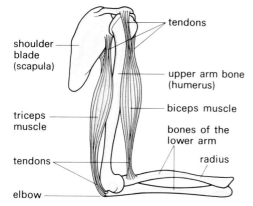

tendons

shoulder
blade
(scapula)

upper arm bone
(humerus)

biceps muscle

triceps
muscle

bones of the
lower arm

tendons

radius

elbow

Fig. 13.49

Name muscles A and B in Fig. 13.48. Move the 'bones' in the model arm. Which muscle becomes shorter and fatter when the arm moves upwards? What happens to the shape of the other muscle?

1 the biceps muscle contracts;
2 the radius bone is pulled upwards, because the muscle is attached to it by a tendon;
3 the triceps muscle is pulled into a long thin shape.

However, once the biceps has contracted, it will remain in that position. It cannot get longer by itself and push. How then do you lower your arm? What happens to the forearm when the triceps contracts? Will the biceps change in length after this contraction? If it does how will it change?

Our limbs are moved in this way by pairs of muscles. As one gets shorter or contracts, the other gets longer and thinner. We say that the other muscle has **relaxed**.

13.26 HUMAN LEVERS

Your limbs, especially your arms, act as a system of levers. Think of your arm as a lever. What do you think acts as the pivot of the lever?

Experiment 13.22

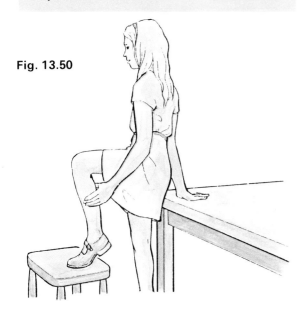

Fig. 13.50

Look at Fig. 13.50. Hold the calf of your leg in a similar way. Lift your heel, keeping your toes on the ground. Is the muscle which lifts your heel at the front or back of your leg? Lower your heel. Keeping your heel on the ground, lift up your toes. Which muscle pulls when the toes are lifted? Together these two muscles, just like the two that lift your forearm, form a pair of muscles.

13.25 HOW DO MUSCLES MOVE YOUR LIMBS?

Muscles work by getting shorter or **contracting**. Look again at Fig. 13.49. When the forearm is moved up the following things happen:

Fig. 13.51

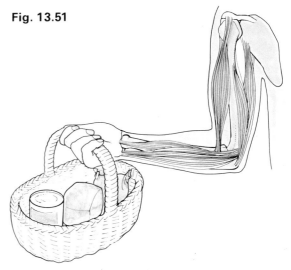

Figure 13.51 shows the bones and muscles at the elbow joint of an arm holding a basket. Which muscle produces the effort force? What acts as the load force?

WHAT YOU HAVE LEARNT IN THIS UNIT

1 Forces can change the shape, speed, and direction of movement of a body.
2 Friction is a force which resists movement.
3 The force of friction varies according to the materials rubbing together and can be reduced by lubrication and by ball bearings.

4   The Earth's pull on objects is called gravity. Weight is a measure of the pull of gravity on an object.

5   The unit of force is the newton. On Earth a mass of 1 kg has a weight of about 10 newtons.

6   Levers and pulleys enable a small force to overcome a bigger one, but the applied force travels a much greater distance than the load does.

7   Work done can be measured by multiplying the force applied by the distance through which it moves.

8   Some energy is wasted as heat in all machines, mainly in overcoming friction.

9   The turning effect of the force on a lever is equal to the size of the force times its distance from the pivot.

10 Liquids transmit forces more effectively than gases.

11 Forces always occur in pairs. There is always a reaction or recoil force equal to the force applied.

12 Your skeleton, which is found inside you, is made up of many bones.

13 The skeleton provides support and protection and allows movement.

14 Animals which have no internal skeleton (invertebrates) have firm or hard skins which act like skeletons.

15 Land plants are kept upright by strong woody fibres in their stems. Some, usually young seedlings, are supported by water in their cells.

16 Our limbs bend at joints.

17 We use muscles to move. The muscles that move our limbs occur in pairs. A muscle works by getting shorter or contracting. It becomes longer only as a result of being pulled out when its paired muscle contracts. When one muscle has contracted, its partner, which is long and thin, is said to be relaxed.

NEW WORDS YOU HAVE MET IN THIS UNIT

compress   to squeeze into a smaller space.

compressibility   the ease with which anything can be squeezed into a smaller space.

contraction   (of a muscle)   shortening of a muscle to produce movement.

force   a push, pull, or twist.

friction   a force which opposes the movement of one surface over another.

gravity   the force with which one body attracts another, particularly, for example, the force which draws bodies towards the Earth.

joint   part of a limb where bending takes place.

mass   the amount of stuff in anything.

muscle   an organ of the body that contracts and produces movement.

newton   the unit in which force is measured.

relaxation (of a muscle)   the pulling of a muscle by its 'muscle partner' until it is long and thin (the opposite of contraction).

skeleton   the supporting structure of an animal.

spine   the central supporting column of the skeleton.

tendon   tissue which connects a muscle to a bone.

weight   the force with which anything is attracted towards the Earth.

SOME QUESTIONS FOR YOU

1   Friction is a force which opposes motion of one thing over another. Yet friction is essential for a car to move along the road. Explain this.

2   Which parts of a bicycle should be oiled to reduce friction? Which parts make use of the force of friction and should never be oiled?

3   What is the minimum depth of tread required by law on a car tyre? Why is this required?

4

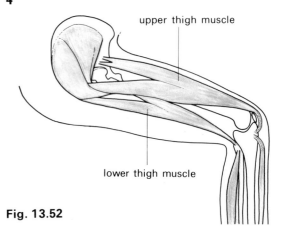

Fig. 13.52

Which muscle contracts when the leg is straightened?
Which muscles relax?
How many joints are shown in the diagram?

5   Try to find the position of the muscles which open and close your mouth (i.e., move your lower jaw). Draw a simple diagram to show where they are.

Transport systems

14.1 WHAT ARE TRANSPORT SYSTEMS?

As soon as you hear or read the word 'transport', you probably think of cars, buses, lorries, trains, and aeroplanes. They carry, or **transport**, people and goods from one place to another. If you look out of the window you may see cars, buses, and lorries. The road outside your school is only one of a large system of roads, which includes motorways, main roads, and side streets. Traffic on motorways is travelling quickly from one place to another. Traffic on smaller roads is moving away from the main trunk road to its destination. The whole arrangement of roads is called a **transport system**. Goods and people are carried, or 'transported' along these roads from one place to another. In a similar way there is, in most countries, a network of railways for transporting goods and passengers from one part of the country to another.

Although travelling from one place to another by road or rail is very important in our everyday lives, it is not really as important as the transport systems in our bodies. What is carried from one place to another in your body? Food, oxygen from

the air, and waste products which are the remains of the food you have eaten or are produced when the food you have eaten is used to give energy.

In this Unit you will find out how these materials are transported from one part of your body to another. By the end of the work you will probably be impressed by the wonderful way in which you are made and in which you function.

14.2 TYPES OF FOOD

Do you remember learning a little bit about food in Unit 3? There are a number of basic kinds or classes of substances which make up our food. These are carbohydrates, proteins, fats, vitamins, and mineral salts. Carbohydrates include starch and sugars.

There are actually quite a lot of substances which are called sugar. There is the sugar that you put in your tea, called cane sugar or beet sugar (according to whether it comes from sugar cane or sugar beet), there is milk sugar, which is found in milk; fruit sugar, which is found in many fruits; and glucose, which is found in many plants and animals. These are just a few of the many different sugars.

Fig. 14.1 A transport system. Can you relate this to your own body and the movement of liquids around it?

Everything you eat can be grouped or classified under one or more of the basic classes of food. Carbohydrates, proteins, fats, vitamins, and mineral salts all play an important part in keeping you fit and healthy. You will discover later in this Unit what each does. First you must discover how to test for the presence of each of these substances in the foods you eat.

Experiment 14.1
Testing foodstuffs

Your teacher will give you four test-tubes, A, B, C, and D. Tube A contains starch, B contains glucose, C contains a protein, D contains oil – a fat. Place your tubes in a test-tube rack so that you can see the labels clearly. Add one dropperful of iodine to each tube. What colour changes do you see?

Take a Clinistix (**be careful** – do not touch the coloured paper at the end of the strip). What colour is it? Dip the strip into each tube, using a new strip each time. What colour is the paper after each test?

Take an Albustix. What is the colour of the paper at the end of the strip? Dip the Albustix into each tube as you did with the Clinistix. What colour is the paper after each test?

Rub a few drops of liquid from each tube onto a filter paper. Dry the paper. What do you see?

Record your results in a table like the one below.

Foodstuff	Substance or reagent used to test foodstuff (testing substance)	Initial colour or appearance of testing substance	Final colour or appearance of testing substance
Starch			
Glucose			
Protein			
Fat			

Look at your results. You have found a quick and easy way to test for each class of foodstuff.

Iodine changes from brown to blue-black when starch is added. The pink paper on a Clinistix goes purple when glucose is present. The yellow paper on an Albustix goes green when a protein is present. A greasy stain is left on dried filter paper by a fat.

You are now going to use these **food tests** to find out what the foods you usually eat contain.

Fig. 14.2

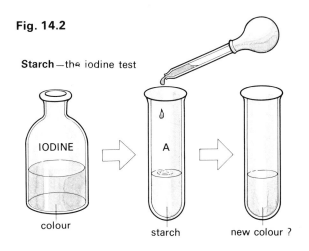

Starch —the iodine test

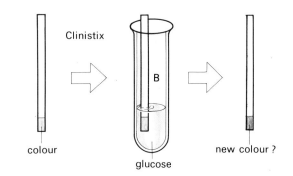

Glucose —the Clinistix test

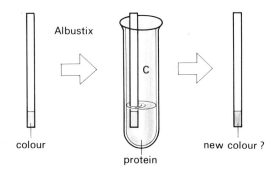

Proteins —the Albustix test

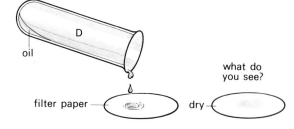

Fats — the filter paper test

Experiment 14.2
What do your foods contain?

Label four test-tubes A, B, C, and D. Grind up some food, for example potato, in a little water. Pour some of the potato juice into each of the four tubes.

Add iodine to tube A. Does it go black? Dip a Clinistix into tube B. Does the paper change from pink to purple? Dip an Albustix into tube C. Does the paper change from yellow to green? Pour a little juice from D onto filter paper. Dry the paper. Has a greasy stain formed?

If the answer to one of these questions is yes, this means that the potato contains that class of food. If the answer is no, then that class of food is missing from the potato.

Test more foods in this way. Enter your results in a table like the one below. Put a tick (√) if the food is present, and a cross (×) if it is absent.

Food in your diet	Starch	Glucose	Protein	Fat
Potato				
Milk				
Cheese				
Crisps				
Apple				

Compare your results with those of other members of your class. From your results, write down examples of food rich in (a) glucose, (b) starch, (c) protein, and (d) fat. Write down examples of foods which are rich in more than one class of food. Why is milk sometimes called a complete food?

14.3 WHY DO WE EAT FOOD?

You eat foods to give you energy, to help you grow, to keep you warm, and to keep you healthy. No single class of food can do all these things for you. Carbohydrates give energy, proteins help growth and healing of cuts and breaks, fats provide warmth and energy. But how do you stay healthy? You need all three main classes of food for this, but you also need small amounts of vitamins and mineral salts. These substances help you to have clear skins, strong bones and teeth. They are contained mainly in fresh fruit and vegetables.

You have learned a lot about foods in this paragraph. See how much you remember by filling in a table like the one below.

Food class	What it does
Carbohydrates (starch and glucose)	
Fats	
Proteins	
Vitamins and minerals	

14.4 A BALANCED DIET

A balanced diet contains the correct proportion of each of the food classes to keep you healthy. If your food contains a lot of carbohydrate and very little protein, it would not be balanced. Many of the meals you choose to eat are certainly not balanced meals. What is wrong with the following meal – pizza, chips, chocolate sponge and coke?

Unfortunately very large numbers of children and their parents do not have the privilege of having balanced meals. In many regions of Africa, India, and South America, the only food available, and often only in small quantities, is rice or maize. These are both carbohydrates. Many people eat no proteins at all. Figure 14.3 shows you the effect of lack of protein on two children.

A balanced diet must also contain bulk. Certain foods, especially fruit and vegetables, contain a substance called **cellulose**. This substance cannot be broken down fully inside you, and so it provides bulk. It forms **roughage**, an important part of your diet. You will find out why it is so important later in the Unit. In addition to all the classes of food, our diet must include water.

Fig. 14.3 These children are suffering from protein deficiency.

eggs

grapes

cheese

ice cream

cream cake

sardines

potatoes

bread

pear

bacon

lemonade

butter

carrots

cereal

fish

pork chop

milk

beans

bananas

Fig. 14.4

1 Collect pictures of food from magazines. Make posters using your pictures to show (a) the main classes of foods (you could have a separate poster for each food class), and (b) a balanced diet.

2 Look at the foods drawn in Fig. 14.4.

(a) Draw a table like the one below. Put the names of the foods in the correct column. The same food may appear in more than one column.

Starch	Glucose	Protein	Fat	Vitamins and minerals
		sardine	sardine	sardine

(b) Select a number of foods for the following different types of meals: a balanced diet for yourself; a meal rich in carbohydrates; a meal for a person who wanted to lose weight and was on a slimming diet; a meal that might be eaten by an athlete during training.

14.5 FEEDING IN ANIMALS

Feel the teeth in your mouth with your tongue. Do they all feel the same shape? How many of them have thin sharp edges? How many are pointed? How many have large, flattish surfaces and feel like double teeth?

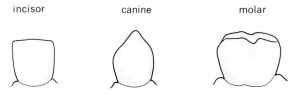

incisor   canine   molar

Fig. 14.5

You have three basic types of teeth. The teeth at the front of your mouth have thin, sharp edges. These are called **incisor** teeth. Your pointed teeth, on each side of the incisors, are called **canines**. The teeth at the back of your mouth with the large flat surfaces are called **molars**. Try to find these teeth in Figs 14.6 and 14.7

Fig. 14.6

Fig. 14.7

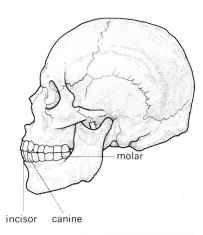

molar

incisor   canine

Experiment 14.3
How many teeth do you have?

Using your tongue or your fingers, count the number of each type of tooth you have. Start with your upper jaw, then count the ones in your lower jaw. Complete a table like the one below.

Type of tooth	Number in upper jaw	Number in lower jaw	Total
Incisor			
Canine			
Molar			
		Total number of teeth	

The kinds and number of teeth you have is called your **dentition.**

Experiment 14.4

Bite a piece of bread. Which teeth did you use? Now chew the bread. Which teeth did you use? Bite off a small lump of toffee from a toffee bar. Did you use the same teeth to bite the toffee as you did to bite the bread?

You probably used your incisors to bite the bread, and the more pointed canines to bite the toffee. You chewed both with the large molars at the back of your mouth. Incisors and canines are biting and tearing teeth. Molars are chewing teeth.

14.6 TOOTH STRUCTURE

Your teeth are not solid lumps of white bone, as they might appear. Figure 14.8 shows you what you would see if you cut a tooth down its length and looked inside.

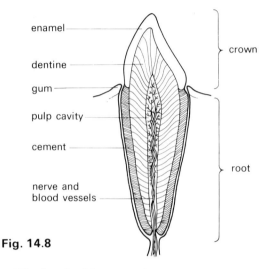

Fig. 14.8

The hard white outer layer is called **enamel**. This protects an inner layer of material called **dentine**. In the centre of the tooth is a space or cavity called the **pulp cavity**. It contains blood vessels and nerves. When you have a tooth pulled out, your gum bleeds because the blood vessels in the pulp cavity have been torn. If a hole forms in your tooth because of decay, air reaches the nerves in the pulp cavity and gives you toothache.

14.7 CARE OF TEETH

Our teeth, although very important to us, are often neglected. Are all your teeth in perfect condition or have you had some filled or pulled out by your dentist?

Experiment 14.5

Count the total number of healthy incisors you have, first in your top jaw, then in your bottom jaw. If you have difficulty doing this a friend can help. Now count how

---

many incisors you have that are damaged, filled, or missing. Do this for your canine teeth, and then for your molars. Complete a table like the one below.

	Incisors		Canines		Molars	
	H	D	H	D	H	D
Upper jaw						
Lower jaw						
Total						

H = healthy teeth   D = damaged, decayed, or missing teeth

Do you have perfect teeth? Compare your results with those of other pupils in your class. You could draw a graph to show the results of each person in your class, and compare your survey with those carried out by other classes. How many pupils in your year have got perfect teeth? It has been estimated that in this country only two people in every hundred have perfect teeth. If you did a similar survey of Eskimos' teeth, or of chimpanzees' teeth, you would find quite different sets of results. Can you think why this should be so? Do you think it might have something to do with what they eat? Before you can answer this you must find out what causes tooth decay.

Experiment 14.6
What causes tooth decay?

Take a tooth, a pig's or a sheep's tooth will do, and dip it into molten wax. Allow the wax to harden, then scrape away a small strip of wax from the surface of the tooth. Place the tooth in a dish of dilute acid so that it is completely covered. After a few days, remove the tooth and scrape away all the remaining wax. Prod the tooth with a needle, first in the area that was not protected by wax, then in the area that was covered. Is the unprotected enamel still hard, or has it become soft?

14.8 PREVENTION OF TOOTH DECAY

There are two ways of reducing tooth decay. You can remove the cause of the decay, and you can strengthen the teeth. Brushing your teeth regularly removes the sticky particles between them, as well as some of the bacteria on the surface of the teeth. If these are removed acid will not be formed to soften the enamel. It has been found that a naturally-occurring chemical, calcium fluoride, strengthens the enamel of the teeth. It occurs in rocks only in certain parts of the country, and in these areas the drinking water contains fluoride. Children who drink this water have strong enamel on their teeth and so fewer of their teeth decay. Sodium fluoride can be added to drinking water at the waterworks, but many people have fought to prevent this. They argue that they should be able to choose whether or not they take fluoride. Do you agree or disagree with them? Remember that many chemicals are already added to your drinking water. Fluoride is now being added to some toothpastes.

14.9 TEETH IN OTHER MAMMALS

Your hands play an important part in feeding you. When you go home today, put some bread on the table in front of you. Try to eat the bread with your hands behind your back. Have you ever wondered how animals which do not have hands like yours manage to eat? You are going to investigate this problem now.

Experiment 14.7

Look at the skulls of a dog and a sheep. With the help of Fig. 14.9, identify the teeth in each skull.

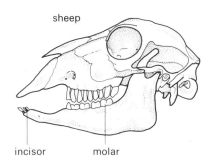

sheep

incisor   molar

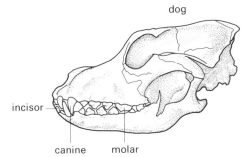

dog

incisor

canine   molar

Fig. 14.9

Run your fingers over the teeth at the back of the sheep's skull. Are these teeth smooth or ridged? Look at the shape of the teeth in the skull and decide how they are used in feeding. When a sheep is chewing grass do the jaws go up and down or from side to side? Hold the lower jaw against the upper jaw and see how the teeth in each jaw fit together. Move the lower jaw from side to side. When a sheep chews grass it makes this action with its jaws.

Look at the dog's skull. The Latin name for a dog is 'canis'. How do you think the canine tooth got its name? Suggest how each type of tooth is used by the dog in feeding. Hold the lower jaw against the upper jaw. Try to move the lower jaw from side to side. Can you do this easily? In what direction do the jaws move when a dog eats?

The sheep is a grass-eating animal (**herbivore**). It bites grass with its incisors and chews it thoroughly with its ridged molars. The dog is a meat-eating animal (**carnivore**). It tears its meat with its canines.

Figure 14.10 shows the skull of an unknown animal which was found in a field. Look at the teeth and decide if the animal was a plant-eater or a flesh-eater. Give reasons for your choice.

Fig. 14.10 What did this animal eat?

14.10 WHERE DOES YOUR FOOD GO?

You have seen how teeth are well shaped to break down food into small enough pieces to go into the mouth. But what happens to food in your mouth? What happens to it when you swallow it? Where does it go? These are just a few of the problems you are now going to investigate.

When you swallow food it passes into a long tube called the digestive canal or the **alimentary canal**.

Figures 14.11, 14.12, and 14.13 show you the alimentary canals of three different animals, a water flea or *Daphnia*, an earthworm, and a mammal.

In *Daphnia* the alimentary canal is a short, simple tube. The alimentary canal of the earthworm looks more complicated, but it is still basically a long tube. Certain regions of the tube have become swollen and thick. In these regions, changes take place in the worm's food.

The alimentary canal of the rat looks very complicated indeed. Look carefully at the diagram. Look for the position of the heart and lungs. These organs, which are found in the chest cavity, are not part of the alimentary canal, but they lie close beside the first part of the digestive tube, the **gullet** or **oesophagus**. Find the **diaphragm**. This is the large sheet of muscle which separates the chest cavity from the abdominal cavity. Most of the alimentary canal is found in the abdominal cavity. Look for the following regions in the diagram: the stomach, the small intestine, the large intestine, and the rectum. These all form part of one long tube. The tube swells out to form the stomach, narrows again to form the small intestine, then it thickens to form the large intestine and the rectum. Because the tube is so long, it is folded up into many loops inside the abdominal cavity. The loops do not flap about inside the animal's body. They are held in position by a tough, clear material found between the loops. When you see a rat being dissected, look for this clear material and the network of blood vessels in it. You will soon understand the importance of these blood vessels.

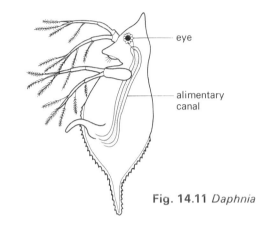

Fig. 14.11 *Daphnia*

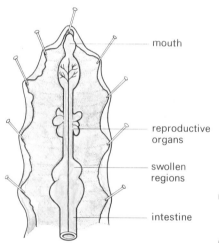

Fig. 14.12 An earthworm

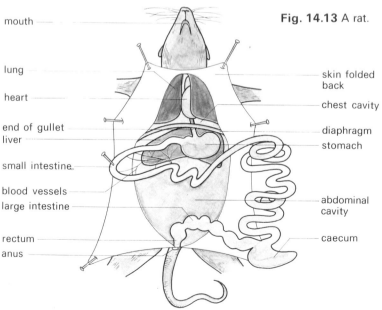

Fig. 14.13 A rat.

Experiment 14.8
Looking inside a rat

Your teacher will cut open a dead rat. With the aid of Fig. 14.13, find the following regions: the mouth, stomach, small intestine, large intestine, rectum, and anus. These are all parts of the alimentary canal. Now look for the liver, the lungs, and the heart. Your teacher will unravel the intestine carefully, and remove the alimentary canal by cutting through the oesophagus and the rectum. When it is laid on a board you will see that it is one long tube.

The large green structure, at the end of the small intestine, is called the caecum (pronounced 'seecum'). It contains bacteria, which digest some of the food in the intestine. Measure the length of the entire alimentary canal.

When the intestine was unravelled, two small tubes were broken. These tubes joined the liver and the pancreas to the intestine. Look for these tubes in Fig. 14.14, a diagram of the human alimentary canal. The liver and pancreas make substances which pass into the intestine and help to break down the food. Similar substances, made by the salivary glands in the head, pass through tubes into the mouth.

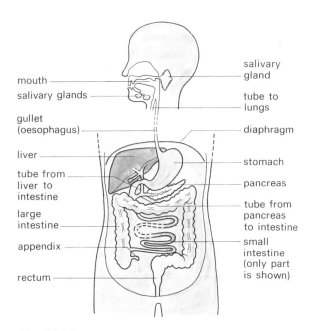

Fig. 14.14

Figure 14.14 is a diagram of the human alimentary canal. It shows the basic shape of the canal. The colours in the diagram are *not* the colours inside you!

14.11 MOVEMENT OF FOOD

Swallow some water. Where does it go when it passes over your throat? How does it travel to your stomach? You might think that it just trickles down your gullet, because of gravity, just like water running from a tap. Is there a volunteer in your class who will try to drink some water while standing on his or her head? Is it possible? How does a giraffe drink water? The following experiment should show you how you and the giraffe can transfer water, against gravity, from your mouth *up* to your stomach.

Experiment 14.9

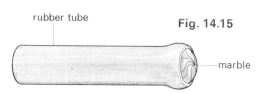

Fig. 14.15

Your teacher will give you a piece of rubber tubing and a glass marble which just fits into one end of the tube.

How can you make the marble travel through the tube to the opposite end, using only your fingers?

If you 'pinch' or squeeze the rubber tube just behind the marble, the marble moves along.

Food is pushed along your alimentary canal in a similar way. When a lump of food is forced over your throat by your tongue, it stretches the muscles in the wall of the gullet. The muscles then contract behind the food and push it down. In this way food is pushed by a series of muscular contractions along the length of the alimentary canal. The muscles of the intestine work best if bulky food is present, and that is why roughage is important in our diet. The process by which food is moved down your alimentary canal is called **peristalsis**.

14.12 DIGESTION

Food spends about 24 hours in your alimentary canal. What happens to it there?

Experiment 14.10

Shake up some bread, potato, rice, or other food rich in starch, in water. Does it dissolve? Shake up some powdered glucose in water. Does it dissolve? Most of the foods we eat are insoluble in water, although some, such as glucose, are soluble.

14.13 STARCH AND GLUCOSE

Starch and glucose are both carbohydrates. What tests did you carry out to show the presence of each? (Refer back to Experiment 14.1.) Starch is found in a large number of the foods you eat.

Experiment 14.11

Your teacher will provide you with a strip of a special cellulose-like material called visking tubing. Soak the strip in water until it has softened. Separate the sides of the tube by rubbing it between your fingers. It should now form a tube. Knot one end of the tube. Half fill the tube with the mixture of starch and glucose solution provided. Knot the other end securely. Carefully rinse the outside of the tube with water. Put the tube in a test-tube of water as in Fig. 14.16.

Remove a sample of the *water* from the test-tube. Dip a Clinistix into this sample to test for the presence of glucose. Add iodine to see if starch is present in the sample. Take samples of liquid from the test-tube at two-minute intervals until a further five samples have been removed. Each time test the liquid for the presence of glucose and starch. Enter your results in a table like the one below.

Time	Glucose	Starch
Start		
2 min		
4 min		
6 min		
8 min		
10 min		

From your results, answer the following questions.
1 Which substance, starch or glucose, passed through the tubing?

Fig. 14.16

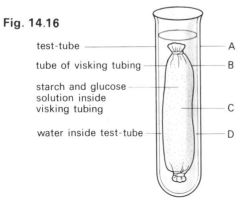

test-tube — A
tube of visking tubing — B
starch and glucose solution inside visking tubing — C
water inside test-tube — D

2 What does this suggest about the walls of the tubing?
3 Why are some molecules able to pass through and others not?
4 Which molecule do you think is larger – starch or glucose?

Visking tubing is a material with extremely small holes in it, too small for us to see. It acts as a sieve, and allows only very small molecules to pass through it. Glucose molecules were able to pass through these holes, but starch molecules were unable to do so. This suggests that glucose molecules are smaller than starch molecules.

The walls of your alimentary canal behave like visking tubing, and only allow small molecules to pass through them. The food that you eat must pass through the walls of the intestine so that it can go into your blood stream. However, most of the food you eat contains large complex molecules, such as starch. These molecules are too big to pass through the walls of your intestine into your blood vessels. In the intestine these large complex molecules are broken down into molecules small enough to pass through the walls. This breaking down process is called **digestion**.

Experiment 14.12

Close your eyes, and think of your favourite food. Imagine you are chewing it slowly. What changes happen in your mouth?

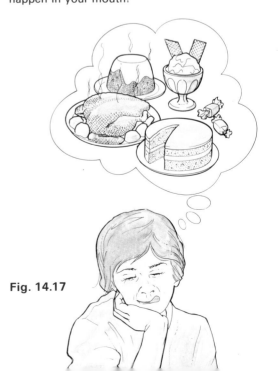

Fig. 14.17

You should find that your mouth has filled with saliva. This is a very important liquid. It keeps your mouth moist (you will soon find out why this is important) and it contains a special juice, called a digestive juice, which begins the breakdown of starch.

Experiment 14.13
The breakdown of starchy foods by saliva

Chew a piece of dried bread for five minutes. What does the bread feel like after this time? Do you notice any change in the taste? Collect some saliva from yourself and your partner. Put about 2 cm depth of starch solution into a test-tube. Add some saliva, and shake the tube well for five minutes. Test the liquid in the tube with a Clinistix. What substance are you testing for? Add iodine to the liquid. What substance are you testing for this time? What do you think the saliva does to starch?

Experiment 14.14
Another starch and saliva experiment

Half fill a beaker with water at about 37 °C (body temperature), or use a water bath set at this temperature. Label two white tiles A and B. Place separate drops of iodine onto each tile. Label two test-tubes A and B. Pour about 2 cm depth of starch solution into each.

Collect some saliva from yourself and your partner. Mix it with an equal amount of water and add it to tube A only. Stand tubes A and B in the beaker of warm water

and start a stop-clock or note the time. Put a clean dropper into each tube. After one minute remove a sample from each tube. Add the sample from A to the first drop of iodine in tile A, and the sample from B to the first drop of iodine in tile B. Note the colour produced in each. Repeat this every minute for five minutes, or until you get a colour change. Figure 14.18 shows you a summary of this experiment. Complete a table like the one below.

Time	Result of test	
	A	B

Here are some questions for you to answer.
1 After five minutes, what colour did the iodine turn in A?
2 Is starch still present in tube A?
3 After five minutes, what colour did the iodine turn in B?
4 Is starch still present in tube B?
5 Explain any difference in colour in tubes A and B.

Now test the liquid in each tube with a Clinistix. Answer the next set of questions.

1 What does this show?
2 What does saliva do to starch?
3 Compare Experiments 14.13 and 14.14. Why was tube B set up in Experiment 14.14?
4 What do we call tube B?
5 Suggest another control which could have been used in this experiment. What would this control show?

Fig. 14.18

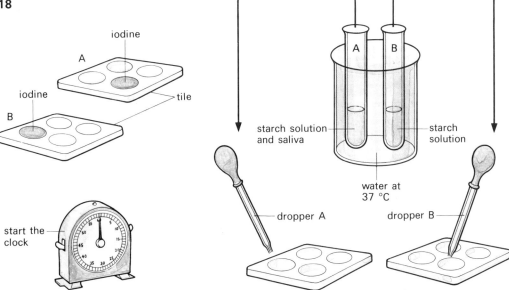

The large starch molecules in tube A were broken down, or digested, into small sugar molecules by the digestive juice in saliva. This juice is one of a large group of **enzymes** found in the body. Enzymes are very important substances. They speed up chemical reactions in organisms, but they themselves remain unchanged. We should be very different persons – if we could live at all – if there were no such things as enzymes. Each particular enzyme has a special job to do; and there are plenty of jobs to be done inside us.

It would be interesting to find out whether enzymes are able to work at any temperature, or if there is one temperature at which they work best.

Experiment 14.15
Do enzymes work at different temperatures?

In Experiment 14.14 you used water at a temperature of 37 °C. Does the enzyme in saliva digest starch at other temperatures? Find this out for yourself. Use temperatures both below and above 37°C.

14.14 WHAT HAPPENS TO FOOD IN YOUR ALIMENTARY CANAL?

As you have found, your alimentary canal can be divided into five basic regions, mouth, gullet, stomach, small intestine, and large intestine. Here is a brief look at what happens to food in each region.

In the **mouth**, food is chewed to break it up and moistened with saliva. Saliva contains a digestive juice which begins to break down large starch molecules. Saliva also moistens food so that you can swallow it.

Experiment 14.16

Close your mouth and swallow. Immediately afterwards swallow again, then again. How many times can you swallow? Can you swallow when your mouth is dry?

Food is pushed from your mouth to your **gullet**. It moves down your gullet by peristalsis to your stomach.

The **stomach** contains a digestive juice and an acid which helps digestion. Your food is broken down further in the stomach, and it then passes into the **small intestine**.

Look back to Fig. 14.14 on page 107. You will see that the small intestine is a long thin tube. This is the main region for digestion. What do you think is the importance of the length of this tube? Figure 14.19 shows a cross section of the small intestine.

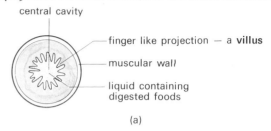

(a)

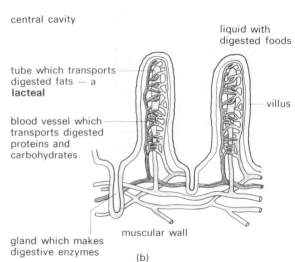

Fig. 14.19 (a) Cross-section of a villus. (b) Longitudinal section of the wall of the small intestine.

The finger-like projections, called **villi**, greatly increase the surface area of the intestine. There are three different kinds of juices in the intestine. Each is produced in a different part of the body. The first juice is made by special cells in the wall of the small intestine (Fig. 14.19). The second is made by the pancreas and passes through a tube, called the pancreatic duct, into the small intestine. (Fig. 14.14). The third is called bile. Bile is made in the liver, and passes into the small intestine through the bile duct.

Your food spends a long time in your small intestine, and digestion is completed there. The molecules in the digested food are now small enough to pass through the walls of the intestine. Look again at Fig. 14.19. Where do you think the digested food goes? Digested carbohydrates and proteins pass into the blood capillaries. Digested fats pass into the **lacteals**. The lacteals form part of a network of tubes which eventually joins with the blood system. The movement of digested foods across the walls of the small intestine into the blood system is called **absorption**.

Substances, such as cellulose from fruit and vegetables (roughage), which have not been digested in the small intestine, pass into the **large intestine**. This region does not produce enzymes, and no digestion takes place in it. Water is absorbed, through the walls, from the undigested food. The semi-solid remains, the **faeces**, pass into the muscular end of the large intestine called the **rectum**. They are then expelled through the **anus**.

The food is therefore separated into two parts. The digested foods are absorbed through the walls of the intestine into the blood stream. The undigested food travels the entire length of the alimentary canal and leaves the body through the anus.

14.15 TRANSPORT AGAIN

This Unit started by looking at transport systems in general. Do you remember the system of motorways, main roads, and side streets?

When digested foods pass through the walls of the small intestine, they enter a very large and complex system, the **blood system**. Blood carries food away from the intestine. Do you remember seeing blood vessels in the clear tissue between the loops of the small intestine in the rat? All the digested food which passes through the walls of our small intestine is carried to the liver. Much of the food stays in the liver, where it is stored until the body needs it.

The main transport systems of this country are shown in maps. You can look at a map and trace routes of motorways and other roads. In the same way, our main transport system, our blood system, can be drawn in the form of a map. Figure 14.20 shows a simplified map or diagram of your blood system.

14.16 YOUR BLOOD SYSTEM

Look at Fig. 14.20. Find the 'road' or connection between the small intestine and the liver. This road is in fact a large blood vessel. Another large blood vessel leaves the liver and travels up the body to the heart. Find the heart in the diagram. The heart is a **pump**, which pushes blood all round the body.

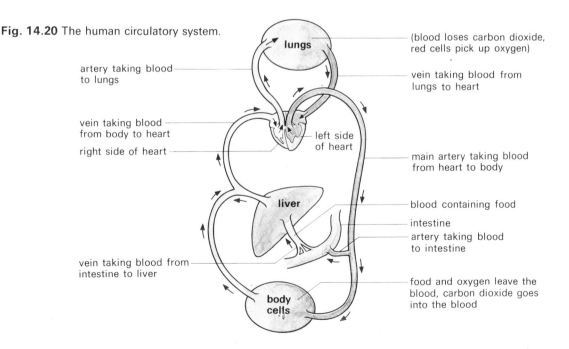

Fig. 14.20 The human circulatory system.

lungs

(blood loses carbon dioxide, red cells pick up oxygen)

artery taking blood to lungs

vein taking blood from lungs to heart

vein taking blood from body to heart

left side of heart

right side of heart

main artery taking blood from heart to body

liver

blood containing food

intestine

artery taking blood to intestine

vein taking blood from intestine to liver

food and oxygen leave the blood, carbon dioxide goes into the blood

body cells

→ direction of flow of blood

Experiment 14.17
The heart

Your teacher will show you a sheep's heart, and the tubes which carry blood into it and away from it. The white material lying on the heart is fat. When the fat is cut away, examine the heart. What colour is it? Can you see any blood vessels on the surface? Feel the two small, pouch-like structures at the top of the heart, then feel the bottom of the heart. Which end feels thicker?

Your teacher will cut open the right side of the heart. How many cavities, or chambers can you see? Are the walls of the cavities the same thickness? What do you see between the chambers? The small upper chamber is called an **auricle**.

Blood which has been round the body, including the blood from the liver, passes into this auricle. The blood passes from the auricle, through a valve into the lower chamber, the **ventricle**. Look at the valve between the auricle and the ventricle. This valve is composed of three flaps of very tough skin, held securely by strong fibres to the muscular wall of the ventricle. Try to lift these flaps with a blunt seeker. Can you lift them right up into the auricle?

The ventricle is muscular and when it contracts it pushes blood upwards. The blood pushes up the flaps until the valve is closed. The tough fibres which anchor the flaps prevent the valve opening into the auricle, and makes the blood flow in one direction only. If the blood does not pass back into the auricle, where does it go? Feel inside the right ventricle with a blunt seeker. You should find a hole at the top end. Push the seeker through the hole. Where does it go? You should see the seeker coming out of the heart through a tube. This tube is a blood vessel which takes blood away from the heart.

Where does this blood go to? Look back at Fig.

14.20. You can see the blood vessel leaving the right side of the heart takes blood to the **lungs**.

This blood has been all round the body. From your work in Unit 8, you will know that this blood will be rich in carbon dioxide, and low in oxygen. In the lungs, the blood loses some of this carbon dioxide, and picks up oxygen. You have already examined lungs. They are just like two sponges, and contain few, if any, muscles. Do you think that they could pump blood all round the body? No, blood from the lungs must pass back to the main pump of the body, the heart.

Blood rich in oxygen returns to the left side of the heart, to the left auricle. Look inside the left side of the heart. How many chambers do you see? Look for a valve. How many flaps does this valve have? This valve serves the same purpose as the one you saw on the right side of the heart. It makes the blood flow in one direction. Find where blood leaves the left ventricle. The large tube leaving the left ventricle carries blood on its long journey round the body. Look for this blood vessel in Fig. 14.20. The heart is in fact two pumps joined together. The right side of the heart pumps blood to the lungs. The left side pumps blood to the rest of the body.

Blood vessels which carry blood away from the heart are called **arteries**. Blood returns to the heart through **veins**.

14.17 ARTERIES AND VEINS

When the heart pumps blood into an artery, the blood is pushed out under pressure. The walls of the arteries are thick to withstand this pressure.

Fig. 14.21 The heart as a pump.

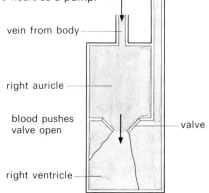

vein from body

right auricle

blood pushes valve open — valve

right ventricle

Blood passes from right auricle to right ventricle.

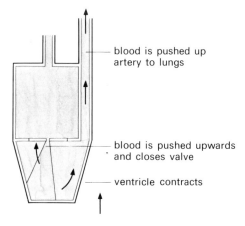

blood is pushed up artery to lungs

blood is pushed upwards and closes valve

ventricle contracts

Right ventricle contracts and pushes blood out of the heart to the lungs.

⟶ Direction of flow of blood

Veins, on the other hand, have much thinner walls. Can you think why? Some veins run from the tip of your toes, up your legs and trunk to your heart. Measure the distance between your toes and your heart. Blood in these veins will have to travel that distance against gravity. What must be present in veins to stop the blood falling back? Similar structures prevented blood being pushed between the ventricles and the auricles. Can you think what keeps blood flowing in one direction in the arteries? One other difference between arteries and veins is that blood rich in oxygen flows through the arteries and blood with less oxygen in it flows through veins.

Experiment 14.18

Your teacher will give you some fresh blood from a cow or a sheep. Put some of this blood into each of two beakers. Bubble oxygen into the blood in one beaker, and carbon dioxide into the blood in the other beaker. Look at the colour produced in each beaker.

Blood rich in oxygen is bright red, whereas blood rich in carbon dioxide is purplish-red.

Complete a table like the one below to show some differences between arteries and veins. One difference has already been filled in.

Arteries	Veins
carry blood from heart	carry blood to heart

Experiment 14.19

Bare your right arm. Grip the arm tightly, just above the elbow, while your right hand grips tightly on to a metre stick or piece of wood. Look at the veins on your arm. You should see lumps appearing on these blood vessels. Can you suggest what these might be? Suggest a reason why they have formed.

The experiment you have just carried out was first performed many years ago by William Harvey. Find out when he lived and why his investigations of the flow of blood round the body were so important.

Experiment 14.20
Your heart and exercise

Sit still on your seat for a few minutes. Find your pulse by placing two or three fingers of one hand (do not use your thumb) on to the opposite wrist. Count the number of times your pulse beats in one minute. Write down your pulse rate at rest. Touch your toes ten times. Take your pulse after this gentle exercise. Now do some vigorous exercise. If your partner holds your stool, you can step on and off it ten times, or you can run around the playground. Take your pulse after this vigorous exercise. Enter your results in a table like the one below.

	Pulse rate (beats per min)
At rest	
After gentle exercise	
After vigorous exercise	

What happens to your pulse as a result of exercise? Why do you think this happens? (Your work in Unit 8 should help you to answer this.)

When you exercise vigorously, your body requires more oxygen to help in energy release. Carbon dioxide is produced at a faster rate, and your body must get rid of this extra carbon dioxide. The heart therefore beats faster than when you are at rest. This makes the blood go at a faster rate through your lungs, where gas exchange takes place.

14.18 CAPILLARIES

The large arteries and veins in your body act like motorways and carry blood quickly in one direction, from one part of the body to another. Smaller blood vessels act like main roads and move blood between the large arteries and veins and the organs of your body. In these organs, the blood vessels become even smaller, so small they are like minute hairs. These very small blood vessels are called **capillaries**. The capillaries have very thin walls, so many substances, such as digested foods, oxygen, and carbon dioxide, can pass through them. You can see the relationship between arteries, veins, and capillaries by seeing what happens in part of the skin (Fig. 14.22).

The artery bringing blood from the heart divides up into a series of smaller tubes which enter the skin. In the skin these tubes divide again and again until they form capillaries. Oxygen and food passes from the blood, through the walls of the capillaries, into the cells in the skin. Carbon dioxide passes in the opposite direction, from the cells in the skin into the blood in the capillaries. The capillaries reunite to form larger tubes which eventually become veins. The veins take blood back to the heart.

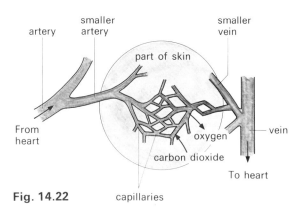

Fig. 14.22

Experiment 14.21
Blood

Spin a sample of fresh blood in a centrifuge for five minutes. Look at the straw-coloured liquid at the top of the sample. This liquid is called **plasma**. Plasma carries food, carbon dioxide, and other waste products around the body. Heat, which is produced mainly in our muscles, is also spread throughout the body by blood.

Using a dropper, remove the plasma from the tube. The dark red layer remaining contains blood cells. Why were they found at the bottom of the tube after the blood had been centrifuged?

Take three clean glass slides. Put a *very small* drop of blood on two of them. Using the other slide, quickly spread or smear the blood over the slides as shown in Fig. 14.23.

Examine the blood smear on one of the slides under the microscope. (You will probably need to use high power.) Draw what you see.

The small round cells are **red blood cells**. They are red because they contain a substance called **haemoglobin**. Haemoglobin takes up oxygen. As the red blood cells pass through the capillaries in the lungs, oxygen is picked up by the haemoglobin – rather like a lorry picking up a load. The red cells carry the oxygen to all cells in the body.

Add a drop of Leishmann's stain to your second blood smear and leave the stain on the slide for about five minutes. Rinse excess stain from the slide with water, then examine the stained smear under the microscope. Draw what you see.

The large, irregular-shaped cells are **white blood cells**. These cells protect us by killing bacteria which enter our bodies. Figure 14.24 shows both types of blood cells.

Fig. 14.23

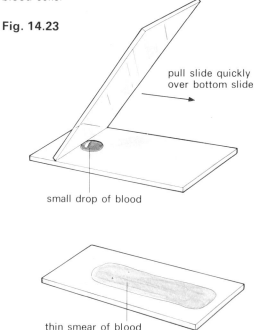

Fig. 14.24 (a) Red blood cells; (b) white blood cells.

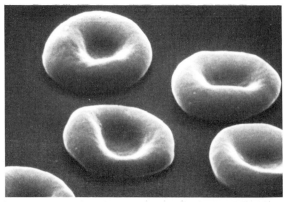

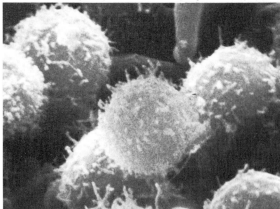

14.19 TRANSPORT IN PLANTS

In Unit 8 you found that in daylight, green plants build up carbon dioxide from the air and water from the soil into glucose and starch. This process is called **photosynthesis**. Can you remember in which part of the plant photosynthesis takes place?

Water enters the plant through its roots and is used in the leaves. How does it get there? Food is made in the leaves, but used in all parts of the plant. Plants must therefore have a transport system so that substances can move freely from one part to another.

Experiment 14.22

You will need some small cress seedlings. Carefully place one in a drop of dilute iodine solution on a microscope slide. Look at the root with a hand lens, or under the low power of the microscope. Is the root smooth or hairy? Are the hairs all along its length or just in certain parts? Draw the root and label the parts. Figure 14.25 will help you to do this.

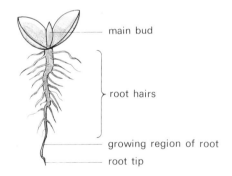

main bud

root hairs

growing region of root

root tip

Fig. 14.25

There are many long finger-like outgrowths on the root. These are the **root hairs**. They are found just behind the growing region of the root. They do not grow on the older parts of the root. Water and mineral salts pass from the soil into the root hairs. The hairs are important to the plant because they greatly increase the area of the root that can absorb water.

Water enters the plant through the root hairs and moves up the root and stem to the leaves. In the next experiment you will try to follow some water taking this journey. Unfortunately water is colourless and you cannot see it inside a plant, so you will have to use coloured water.

Experiment 14.23

Your teacher will give you some plant material, possibly some celery or a leek, which has been standing in coloured water. Cut across the stem. Using a hand lens, look at the cut end. Draw a diagram to show the places where you clearly see the dye. Cut the stem lengthwise, and again look for any signs of colouring. Draw what you see. Was the colour spread evenly throughout the stem, or was it found only in certain areas?

The areas stained with dye show the position of tubes through which the water travelled.

Look at a whole plant that has been standing in coloured water for a day. Find the coloured tubes in the root, the stem, and the leaves. These show the path taken by water as it moves through the plant.

Food travels through a series of similar tubes from the leaves to all parts of the plant. Both sets of tubes form part of the transport system of the plant. Figure 14.26 shows you part of this system.

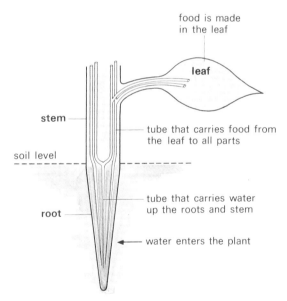

food is made in the leaf

leaf

stem

tube that carries food from the leaf to all parts

soil level

tube that carries water up the roots and stem

root

water enters the plant

Fig. 14.26

14.20 WATER IN PLANTS

Water passes from the soil to the leaves, where some of it is used to make food. What happens to the rest of the water?

Experiment 14.24

Take a small piece of dry cobalt chloride paper. What colour is it? Using a dropper, put one drop of water onto the paper. What colour does the paper turn?

Cut two strips of dry cobalt chloride paper. Attach them with sticky tape to a leaf of a well watered plant. Start a stop clock, or note the time when the paper was attached. Look at the colour of the paper at five-minute intervals, until about thirty minutes have passed. What happens to the paper? What does this tell you?

Fig. 14.27

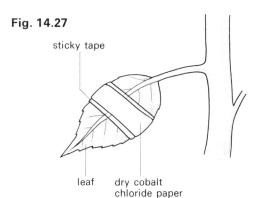

sticky tape

leaf   dry cobalt
        chloride paper

Experiment 14.25

Cover a well-watered plant with a dry polythene bag. Seal the base of the bag carefully with string.

Fig. 14.28

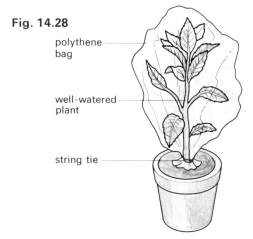

polythene bag

well-watered plant

string tie

Look at the bag after thirty minutes. What has happened to the inside of the bag? What do you think this liquid is? Check your answer by experiment. Where has this liquid come from?

The results of Experiments 14.24 and 14.25 demonstrate that water escapes from the leaves of plants. Leaves have a large number of very small holes in them. Extra water from inside the leaves evaporates, passes through these holes, and goes into the atmosphere.

Water leaves a plant by evaporation from the leaves. In Unit 5 you studied evaporation. Look at the following list of conditions and, from your knowledge of evaporation, choose which would cause water to evaporate quickly from leaves.

still air	high temperature
moving air	low temperature
dry air outside leaf	large leaf surface
moist air outside leaf	small leaf surface

When water evaporates from a plant, the temperature of the plant drops. At what time of year is this most important to plants? At what time of year is this evaporation from plants greatly reduced? Give a reason for your answer. Can you think of any disadvantages of evaporation of water from plants?

14.21 WATER IN PEOPLE

You have just found how water enters and leaves a plant. You are now going to look at these processes in people.

Experiment 14.26
Water in and out

Wrap a piece of polythene around one finger and tie it securely. Keep your finger covered while you carry out the first parts of this experiment.

Water in
Your teacher will provide you with a selection of cups, glasses, cans, and bottles. Try to work out how many cups of coffee, glasses of milk, cans of coke, etc., you drank yesterday. Find the volume of each type of container, then work out the total volume of liquid you drank yesterday. Pour this volume of water into a bucket to see how much liquid you drink in one day. This is not the total amount of liquid that you consume. Your food also contains a high percentage of water.

Water out
You usually drink more water than you need, and you must get rid of the excess or you would burst! How do you lose water?

Every time you urinate you get rid of about 300 ml of liquid. How many times did you urinate yesterday? Work out how much liquid was removed from your body by this process. Is this amount more or less than you drank?

Breathe out onto a cold glass. What do you see? What does this tell you about your breath?

Now look back at your finger. Remove the polythene. Is it wet or dry? Where has the water come from?

Water leaves the body in urine, in your breath (as water vapour), and in sweat. When do you sweat most? What happens to your body temperature when you sweat?

14.22 WATER CONTROL

The amount of water we take in each day varies. Some days we may drink much more than others, yet the amount of water actually in our body remains fairly constant. There must be some part of our body which helps to regulate how much water we retain. This is done by our **kidneys**. Figure 14.29 shows you the position of your kidneys and the tubes leading to and from them.

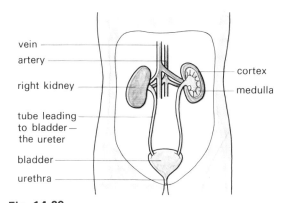

Fig. 14.29

Experiment 14.27

Your teacher will show you a fresh kidney. What colour is it? What does this suggest? Cut the kidney open. With the aid of Fig. 14.30, look for the following regions: artery, vein, cortex, medulla, pelvis, ureter.

Blood enters the kidney through the artery. When it is in the kidney, the blood goes through a process rather like filtration. The blood entering the kidneys contains harmful waste substances,

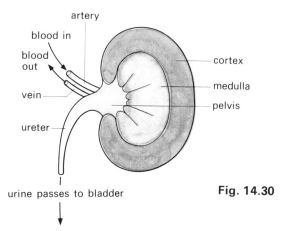

Fig. 14.30

urine passes to bladder

which must be removed. In the cortex of the kidney are millions of fine tubes or 'tubules'. As blood passes through these tubules, the harmful wastes are removed. The waste substances then pass through tubes in the medulla to the ureter, and in this way they leave the kidney. The blood, which now contains fewer impurities, leaves the kidney through the vein. In this way soluble wastes are removed from the blood.

Soluble wastes are not the only substances to pass from the blood into the kidney tubules – water does too. Waste products and water together form **urine**. If your blood contains a lot of water, much of it is removed as the blood flows through the kidneys. It then passes into the ureter. However, if your blood contains too little water, little of it will be removed by the kidneys. If you take in a lot of liquid, then you produce large amounts of dilute urine. If you drink small amounts of liquid, or lose water through sweat, then you produce small amounts of concentrated urine.

Urine passes down the ureters to the bladder. The bladder is a muscular sac which stores urine. At intervals, urine is expelled from a tube, the urethra, which leads to the exterior of the body.

You now know that in your body many complex processes take place. Digested food is carried by the blood to all the cells in the body. Some of this food is broken down by the process of respiration. The oxygen necessary for this reaction is carried by the blood from the lungs to the cells. Energy is released as a result of respiration. Carbon dioxide, the waste product, is carried by the blood from the cells to the lungs. Waste products are carried by the blood, mainly from our liver to the kidneys, where they are filtered out and removed as urine. Blood unites many of the systems in our body. We have a very highly developed, intricate and wonderful transport system.

WHAT YOU HAVE LEARNT IN THIS UNIT

1   Food is made up of carbohydrates, proteins, and fats, together with small amounts of vitamins and mineral salts.

2   You can find out what the food you eat contains by a series of simple food tests.

3   Each class of food plays a part in keeping us fit and healthy. Energy is obtained mainly from carbohydrates and fats; proteins are used for growth and to replace damaged tissues. Vitamins and mineral salts keep us healthy.

4   A balanced diet contains the correct proportion of carbohydrates, proteins, fats, vitamins, and mineral salts. In addition we need roughage to give bulk to our diet, and water.

5   Teeth play an important part in feeding. We have three basic kinds of teeth, each of which acts on food in a different way.

6   Tooth decay is caused by acid produced by the action of bacteria on sticky food trapped between the teeth. It can be reduced by brushing away the food particles and by strengthening the teeth with fluoride, either in the water or in a fluoride toothpaste.

7   The teeth in other animals are adapted to their methods of feeding. Sheep have many ridged teeth for chewing; dogs have pointed teeth to tear up meat.

8   When food is eaten it passes into the alimentary canal, which is a very long tube.

9   Food is pushed along the alimentary canal by a series of muscular contractions called peristalsis.

10   In the alimentary canal food is digested. Large complex molecules are broken down into simple, soluble molecules which can pass through the walls of the small intestine into the blood stream.

11   Enzymes digest foods. Many of these enzymes are made in glands closely connected to the alimentary canal.

12   Enzymes work best at a specific temperature. The enzymes that digest our food work best at body temperature (37 °C).

13   The small intestine is the main region for digestion, and for the absorption of digested foods into the blood stream.

14   The small intestine is well adapted to its functions.

15   The blood system is the main transport system in our body.

16   Blood contains plasma, red blood cells, and white blood cells. Plasma transports digested foods, carbon dioxide, and waste products. Red cells contain haemoglobin which transports oxygen. White cells protect us by killing bacteria.

17   Blood is pumped round the body by the heart. The heart is a double pump. The right side pumps blood to the lungs, the left side to the body. Blood leaves the heart by the arteries and returns to it by the veins.

18   Blood capillaries have thin walls. Substances pass through these walls between the blood and all the cells of the body.

19   Our body produces a number of waste products. Carbon dioxide is removed through the lungs, water is removed in urine and sweat, and solid waste which consists of undigested food is removed as faeces from the anus.

20   The kidneys filter blood and remove impurities from it. These are passed to the bladder as urine. Our kidneys help to control the amount of water in our body.

21   Plants have a transport system. A series of tubes carry water from the roots to the leaves. A different set of tubes distribute food from the leaves to all parts of the plant.

22   Water enters a plant through the root hairs and excess water evaporates from the leaves through many small pores in the leaf surfaces.

NEW WORDS YOU HAVE MET IN THIS UNIT

absorption   movement of digested foods and water through the walls of the intestine into the blood stream.

alimentary canal   tube in the body in which food is digested.

anus   opening at the end of the alimentary canal.

artery   blood vessel that carries blood away from the heart.

auricle   thin-walled chamber at the top of the heart that collects blood

balanced diet   a diet containing the proportions of each class of food, roughage, and water which are best for health.

bladder   a sac that stores urine until it leaves the body.

caecum   part of the alimentary canal of a herbivore that contains bacteria which help in digestion.

canine tooth   tearing tooth.

capillary   very fine blood vessel with thin walls through which substances can pass.

cellulose material found in the walls of plant cells.

dentine inner layer of material in a tooth.

dentition number and kinds of teeth in an animal.

digestion breakdown of large complex molecules into smaller soluble molecules that can be absorbed into the blood stream.

enamel tough protective layer of a tooth.

enzymes substances found in all plants and animals which control many chemical reactions, such as digestion.

fluoride a substance that strengthens the enamel of teeth.

gullet tube which connects the mouth to the stomach.

haemoglobin red pigment, found in red blood cells, which carries oxygen.

heart organ which pumps blood around the body.

incisor a biting tooth.

kidneys organs which filter blood to remove waste, and which help to control the amount of water in the body.

lacteal a tube in the centre of a villus in the small intestine, into which digested fats pass.

large intestine tube leading from the small intestine, into which undigested food passes.

molar grinding or chewing tooth.

pancreas organ of the body, lying near to the stomach, which makes digestive enzymes.

peristalsis series of muscular contractions which move food along the alimentary canal.

plasma straw-coloured liquid part of the blood.

pulp cavity central cavity of a tooth.

rectum short muscular tube at the end of the alimentary canal.

root hair elongated cell in a root into which water passes from the soil.

roughage the bulky part of our diet consisting mainly of cellulose.

saliva digestive juice which acts in the mouth.

salivary glands glands in the face that make saliva.

small intestine main region of the alimentary canal where digestion and absorption take place.

stomach swollen region of the alimentary canal in which food is stored and partly digested.

ureter tube leading from the kidney to the bladder.

urethra tube leading from the bladder, through which urine leaves the body.

urine liquid containing waste products and water that is produced by the kidneys.

vein blood vessel that carries blood to the heart.

ventricle thick-walled chamber at the foot of the heart which pumps blood.

villus finger-like projection in the small intestine. Villi greatly increase the internal surface area of the intestine.

SOME QUESTIONS FOR YOU

1 Look at Fig. 14.16 (page 108). The diagram represents a model of food in the small intestine. Each of the parts labelled A, B, C, and D corresponds to one of the following terms: body wall, blood, gut wall, food.

Write down the letters, and opposite each, the term to which it corresponds.

2 The small intestine is the main region of the alimentary canal for digestion and the absorption of digested foods. List three ways to show how the structure of this tube is suited for these purposes.

UNIT 15

Electrical energy

15.1 LOOKING BACK

You have already done some experiments with electricity in this course (Unit 7, Book 1). In this Unit you are going to find out more about the safe use of electricity at home and at work. As it may be some time since you did any electrical experiments, here are several which will remind you of some important points.

Experiment 15.1
Some revision experiments

(a) Conductors and insulators: using a bulb
Use the apparatus shown in Fig. 15.1. First touch the two loose crocodile clips together. What happens to the bulb? What does this tell you?

The bulb should light, showing that there is a **complete circuit**. This means that electrons can leave the negative end of the cell, pass along through the leads and the bulb, finishing up at the positive end of the cell.

Now separate the clips, and try touching them each against the ends of strips of different material. The bulb will light when you are testing a **conductor**, but will not do so if the material you use is an **insulator** which does not allow electrons to flow through it.

(b) Conductors and insulators: using a bulb and an ammeter
Another way of finding whether a current of electrons is flowing is to use an **ammeter**. By using an extra lead and an ammeter, see if you can connect up both the bulb and the ammeter so that you can try more tests for conductors.

Remove the cell. Show your circuit to your teacher before doing further tests. Be careful to connect the positive (red) terminal of the meter to the positive terminal of the cell. Remember too that you must never connect an ammeter directly across a cell as this would damage it.

An ammeter is connected in series in a circuit and counts the rate at which electrons flow through the circuit. If the ammeter reads 1 amp this means that in each second 6×10^{18} electrons are flowing in the circuit.

To which family of substances do most conductors belong?

By using the bulb and the meter you can test materials which are poorer conductors. These might resist the current so much that the bulb will not light, although the ammeter needle moves.

(c) Voltage and current
In Unit 13 you found out about some common forces. Friction, which is always a resisting force, was one of them. In electricity there is a similar effect when electrons try to flow along a wire. The electrical resistance of the wire is rather like friction; it opposes the flow of electrons. You have to supply an electrical force to push electrons through a circuit against this resistance. This electrical force is called **voltage**, and the instrument used to measure voltage is the voltmeter.

Always connect a voltmeter across a cell (i.e. in

Fig. 15.1

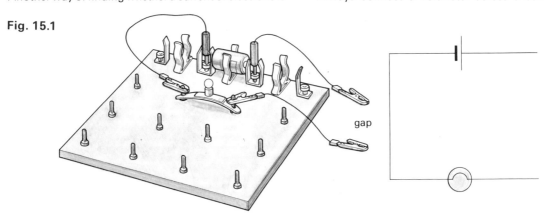

gap

parallel with it) with the positive terminal of the meter connected to the positive terminal of the cell.

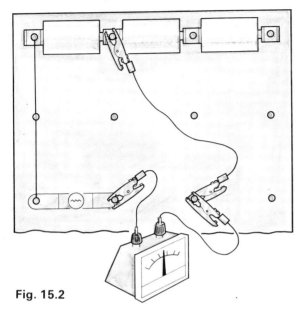

Fig. 15.2

Find the current flowing through each lamp when first one, then two, then three cells are used in series. Each time connect the voltmeter across the cells being used.

You should find that the current flowing when two cells are used is twice that flowing when one cell is used. A battery of twice the voltage pushes twice as many electrons through the circuit in the same time.

15.2 ELECTRICAL ENERGY

Experiment 15.2
Comparing the wattage and brightness of bulbs

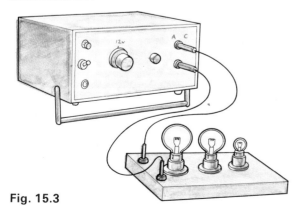

Fig. 15.3

Connect up the circuit shown in Fig. 15.3. The bulbs are in parallel. The bulbs you will use are designed to work from a 12 volt car battery, but a power pack can be used for this experiment. Each bulb is marked with a number in front of the letter W. This tells you the number of watts it consumes.

Switch on the bulbs and notice the brightness of each bulb. Complete a table like the one below.

Bulb	Volts	Watts	Brightness
1	V	W	
2	V	W	
3	V	W	

Which is the brightest bulb?

The bulb which has the highest wattage is the brightest, and it is changing electrical energy into light energy at the fastest rate. Into what other form of energy does it change the electrical energy? Touch the bulb carefully to find out.

Experiment 15.3
Calculating the wattage of a bulb

In this experiment you need a bulb from a car side-lamp and one from a car head-lamp. Both are designed to work from a 12 volt supply, but you are going to use the a.c. terminals of a power pack. The letters a.c. stand for **alternating current** which means that current flows, say, clockwise in our circuit for 1/100th of a second then anti-clockwise for 1/100th of a second. It takes 1/50 second to complete this operation, which is called one cycle. There are 50 of these cycles every second, so the frequency of the mains supply is 50 hertz (Hz).

The power pack is connected to two meters which are rather like those which measure the electrical energy you use at home. They are called **joulemeters** because they measure the electrical energy used in joules. Joule was a British scientist who did a lot of experiments on energy.

To read the scales, note the number on each dial which the hand has just left. The hands on the dials go alternately clockwise and anti-clockwise. Read each meter and write the readings down. Now switch on the power pack for 1 minute 40 seconds (100 s). Switch off the power and read the meter again.

The difference in the readings on each meter tells you how many joules each lamp has used in 100 seconds. Calculate how many joules each bulb used in 1 second. The number of joules the bulb uses per second is called the wattage of the bulb.

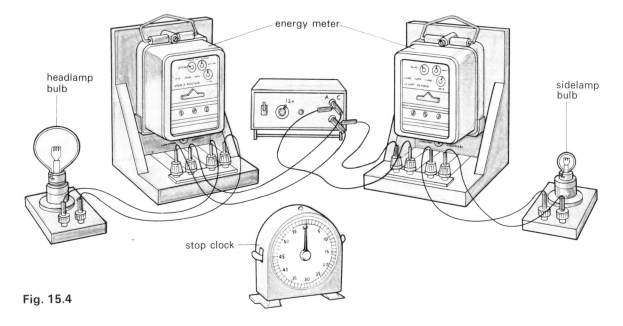

headlamp bulb

energy meter

sidelamp bulb

stop clock

Fig. 15.4

Compare the answer you have put in each case with the number of watts stamped on each bulb. What do you find?

Which bulb used more energy? Which bulb used the energy faster? You have found that the higher the wattage of a bulb the faster it uses energy.

15.3 ELECTRICAL POWER

The **rate** at which energy is changed (in this case from electrical to light) is called the **power**, and it is measured in **watts**. The power of a lamp is simply the number of joules of energy it uses in 1 second. Another way of putting it is to say that 1 joule of energy is used by a lamp of power 1 watt in 1 second.

i.e. power (in watts) = $\dfrac{\text{energy (in joules)}}{\text{time (in seconds)}}$

or energy (in joules)
= power (in watts) × time (in seconds)

15.4 MEASURING ELECTRICAL ENERGY USED AT HOME

At home, with more powerful electrical gadgets and bigger voltages, a bigger unit of energy than the joule is required; in the same way that, if you wanted to measure a long distance between two cities, you would not measure it in metres but in larger units, such as kilometres. This bigger unit of electricity is the quantity of electrical energy that 1000 watts (or 1 kilowatt) would change to heat or some other form of energy in 1 hour. It is called the **kilowatt hour** (abbreviated to kWh) and is often just called a **unit** of electricity.

If you multiply the number of watts in 1 kW by the number of seconds in 1 hour you will find that 1 kWh is 3 600 000 joules.

15.5 THE ELECTRICITY METER

Some modern electricity meters can be read directly from the number they display, but older types may have the dials shown in Fig. 15.5.

This reading is 2509 units

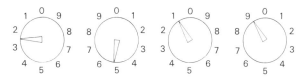

What is the next reading?

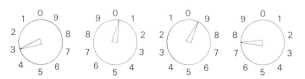

How many units have been used between meter readings?

Fig. 15.5

When current flows through the meter a disc rotates. The more current flowing, the faster the disc turns. It is connected, through gears, to hands which move round circular scales. Look at the electricity meter at your home and ask someone to switch on various appliances. Notice how fast the disc rotates. Does it turn faster when an electric fire is switched on than it does when there is only a single lamp on?

15.6 PAYING FOR ELECTRICAL ENERGY

Find out, by looking at the details stamped on them, the wattages of as many appliances at home as you can.

To find the number of units (kWh) of electricity used, multiply the power in kilowatts by the time in hours for which the appliance is switched on:

number of units (kWh)
= power (in kW) × time (in hours)

Thus in 3 hours a 2 kW heater would use 6 units.

The cost of each unit you use varies according to where you live but on average it will be about 4p or 5p. To get some idea of typical costs answer the following questions, supposing that electricity costs 4p per unit.

1 What is the cost of using a 3 kW heater for 10 hours?

2 What is the cost of using a 150 watt TV set for 4 hours each day this month?

3 What is the cost of using a 5 watt electric clock 24 hours a day for 1 year (365 days)?

15.7 USING ELECTRICITY SAFELY

A warning repeated

In science experiments in school you either use small batteries with low voltage, or a power pack which probably has a voltage of not more than 20 V. You have been warned not to try any experiments at home using mains voltage. The mains supply has a voltage of about 240 V and can send a large, perhaps deadly, current through your body.

In Book 1 you came across two safety devices you must always use with appliances working off the mains. Can you remember what they are?

(a) The earth wire

When wiring up an electric plug you made certain that the green and yellow wire was correctly connected to the earth pin. This is especially important when an electric appliance has a metal case. If any of the insulation on the live lead broke or was torn away, the live wire might touch the metal case. What would happen if you then touched this metal? The current would pass from the metal to your hand, through your body, and into the ground; if you had wet hands this current might kill you.

The earth wire is connected to the metal body and conducts any current which leaks in this way into the earth. It prevents this deadly current passing through you!

(b) The fuse wire

In Book 1 (p. 115) you found that a fuse in series with a light bulb protected the bulb from being burned out. The fuse melted before a current strong enough to have burned out the lamp was reached. The fuse wire was like an automatic switch, and it broke the circuit before damage could be done. You are now going to repeat the experiment on fuses in a little more detail.

Experiment 15.4
A more detailed look at fuse wire sizes

Wind about 0.5 metre of 1 amp fuse wire round a pencil, making it into a coil. Connect this into the circuit as shown in Fig. 15.6. Place a small sheet of polystyrene under the coil. The ammeter should have a range of 0–5 A.

Set the power pack to 0 V and switch it on. Very gradually increase the voltage. What do you see happening to the reading on the ammeter? As you increase the voltage, the current measured by the ammeter should also increase.

Watch the coil of wire carefully. Do you see any change in its appearance as the current increases? It should begin to glow red hot. Keep one eye on the ammeter. What happens to the wire as you increase the current further? Make a note of the biggest current on the ammeter just before the wire 'fuses'.

Now take a reel of 3 A fuse wire. Is this wire thicker or thinner than the 1 A wire? If it is made of the same material it will be thicker.

Make a coil using 0.5 m of 3 A fuse wire and repeat the experiment. What was the current reading on the ammeter just before the wire melted?

Fig. 15.6

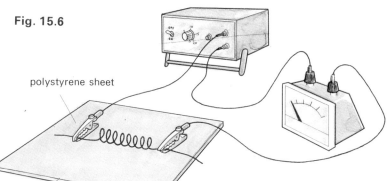

polystyrene sheet

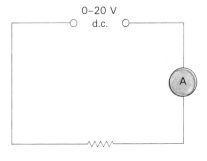

0–20 V
d.c.

A

Fig. 15.7 Different types of fuses.

Do not be surprised if you find that both the 1 A and 3 A fuse wire melt at a higher current than they are supposed to. The cooling effect of the surroundings can have a big effect on when the wire melts. Some fuses in your home are of the cartridge variety. Perhaps you can open up a spare one and have a look at the wire inside – but it cannot be used once you have done so! Ask to be shown the mains fuse box at home; remember that the mains supply has to be **switched off** before you can look inside. You may have some old fuse holders of this type and you can perhaps practice wiring them up with fuse wire.

Experiment 15.5
Another way of finding the wattage of a bulb

In Experiment 15.3 you used joulemeters and a stop-clock to find the wattages of bulbs. Here is another method.

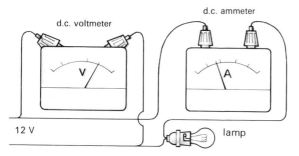

Fig. 15.8

Connect a 12 volt head-lamp in to the circuit shown in Fig. 15.8. Adjust the power pack to 12 volts and switch it on. If the voltmeter does not read 12 volts, adjust the power pack control until it does so. Now take the reading on the ammeter and multiply this number of amps by 12 volts. What number do you get? Is this the number of watts shown on your headlamp bulb, or at least very close to it?

This method of finding the wattage of a lamp gives us the rule

$$\text{power (in watts)} = \text{voltage (in volts)} \times \text{current (in amps)}$$

so $$\text{current (in amps)} = \frac{\text{power (in watts)}}{\text{voltage (in volts)}}$$

15.8 CHOOSING THE CORRECT FUSE

Can you use this rule to find the size of the current in amps which flows through the heating element of a 1000 W fire connected to a mains supply of 250 V? You should find that the current is 4 A.

The common cartridge fuses you can buy are 3 A, 5 A, and 13 A. Which fuse would you use for the fire? The best way to decide is to choose the fuse which is just bigger than the current the appliance requires. In this case you would use a 5 A fuse. When you buy an electric 3-pin plug fitted with a cartridge fuse, it is important to make sure that it is fitted with the most suitable size of fuse.

For a reading lamp using a 100 W bulb the current would be about 0.4 A. Therefore a 3 A fuse would be the most suitable. If a 13 A fuse was fitted it would not melt and switch off the current before the lamp had overheated and a lot of damage was done.

Which fuse would you use for each of the following electrical appliances?

Electrical appliance	Watts	Volts	Amps	Fuse needed
electric fire	1000 W	250 V		
TV set				
kettle				
table lamp				
hair drier				

15.9 MAGNETISM

In Unit 7 you found that the ancient Greeks had been much puzzled by the behaviour of amber when it was rubbed. Sailors in ancient times were equally puzzled by the behaviour of a rock they called 'lodestone'. When they tied a string to a piece of it and hung it up it always pointed towards North. This rock is a natural magnet.

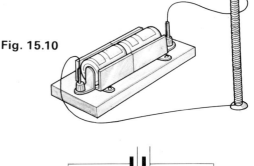

Fig. 15.10

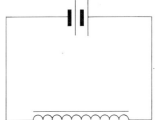

Experiment 15.6
Which objects are picked up by a magnet?

Try to find out which of the following objects can be picked up by a bar magnet.

rubber stopper, copper wire, iron nail, aluminium foil, glass rod, paper clip, steel ball, wooden reel.

You should find that only the objects made of iron or steel are picked up or 'attracted' by the magnet.

Experiment 15.7
An electromagnet

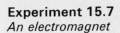

Fig. 15.9

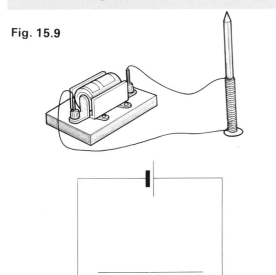

(a) Take about 1 metre of insulated wire and wind it into a neat coil round a 10 cm iron nail. Leave 25 cm of wire free at each end to connect to a cell. With your circuit completed touch one end of the coil against a paper clip. Can you pick up the clip?

Unplug one end of the coil. What happens to the clip now?

You have made an **electromagnet**. You should have found that it is a magnet only when current was flowing in the coil.

(b) Connect the coil to the cell again. This time find out how many small nails the coil can pick up. Now wind more of the free ends of the coil round the nail until only 10 cm of wire is left free at each end to connect to the cell. This will make a longer coil.

Complete the circuit and find out how many small nails the bigger coil can pick up. What is the effect of winding more turns of wire on the coil?

(c) If you use two cells in series the voltage is doubled. Can you remember what effect this has on the current?

Find out how many small nails the coil can pick up if it is connected to two cells. What is the effect of increasing the current on the strength of the electromagnet?

Experiment 15.8
Finding some uses of an electromagnet

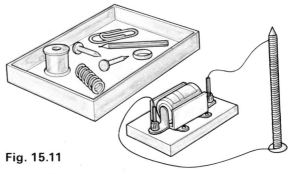

Fig. 15.11

Place a number of small everyday items from your pocket and the laboratory junk box in a small tray. Switch on the electromagnet and use it to lift as many things out of the tray as you can. What do all these things you can lift out have in common?

This experiment suggests a use for electromagnets. They can separate iron and steel objects from different materials. This is the sort of job that metal dealers might have to do in a scrap yard.

Examine any old electric bells, telephone receivers, or telephone 'relays' there may be in the laboratory. They all contain electromagnets. Try to find out how they work.

15.10 THE MOTOR EFFECT

Experiment 15.9
*Can an electric current and a magnet pro-
duce motion?*

Fig. 15.12

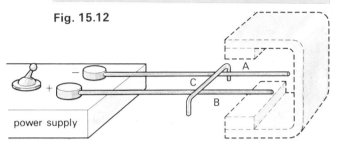

(a) The power pack in this experiment has to be a
special one because, as shown in Fig. 15.12, there
are two copper rods A, and B, connected to the
positive and negative terminals. A third rod, C, with
its ends bent downwards is connected directly
across rods A and B. This will make a very easy path
for the electrons when we switch on, as the copper
rods have practically no resistance. What was this
type of circuit called in Book 1 Unit 7?

You will remember that it was called a **short
circuit**.

The power pack must also supply direct current,
not alternating current. Switch on the supply for
two or three seconds only, and then switch off. Did
anything happen to rod C?

(b) Now place a powerful horseshoe magnet, or a
'yoke' from a Westminster kit, with 2 magnadur
magnets attached, on the open ends of the rods.
(The magnadur magnets should be placed on the
inside of the yoke so that the two sides which
attract are facing each other.) Does anything
happen to rod C when you place the magnet over
the open ends of the rods A and B? Make sure that
no part of the magnet touches the rods. Keeping
the magnet in place, switch on the current for 2 or 3
seconds. Does anything happen to rod C this time?
You should find that it slides along rods A and B as
long as the current is flowing. You have found that
both a current and magnets are needed to make rod
C move.

Next turn the magnet upside down and switch
on the current. What happens to C this time? Now
reverse the direction of the current, so that when
rod C is placed across the rods the current will flow
in the opposite direction. Place the magnet over
the open ends of A and B and switch on the current
for a very short time.

What happens each time you turn the magnet or
reverse the direction of the current? You should

find that in each case rod C is made to move in the
reverse direction.

What made rod C move? It must have been a
force which was produced when a magnet was
brought near a wire which was carrying an electric
current.

(c) **Another way of showing this force**

Fig. 15.13

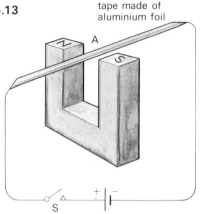

tape made of
aluminium foil

Using the same horseshoe magnet as in part (b),
clamp each end of the aluminium tape (or copper
wire) in a wooden stand. Connect the ends to the
same special power pack and switch it on for a very
short time. What happens? Now reverse the direction of the current by interchanging the ends connected to the power pack terminals. Switch it on
again. What happens? You should find that in one
case the tape (or wire) kicks upwards, and in the
other it kicks downwards.

Can you make up a rule to predict the direction
of the force when the current is switched on?

This force is very important. Its existence
makes life easier for us all. It is the force which
operates in electric motors.

Experiment 15.10
The electric motor

Look at a small electric motor which you can take to
pieces, or one which you can see the inside of. You will
find that it has parts corresponding to those shown in
Fig. 15.14. In the electric motor a coil of wire replaces
the rods you had in your last experiment. This coil is
called an **armature**. The magnets, which, in the motor
you are looking at may be permanent magnets or
electromagnets, are arranged so that when current
flows in the coil one side of the coil is pushed downwards, while the other side is pushed upwards. If this is
all that happened the coil would not keep on turning

Fig. 15.14

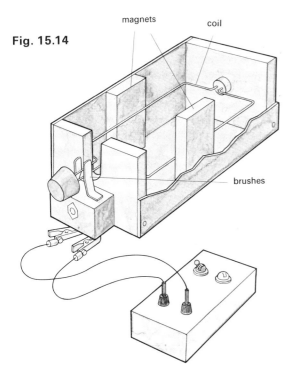

magnets   coil

brushes

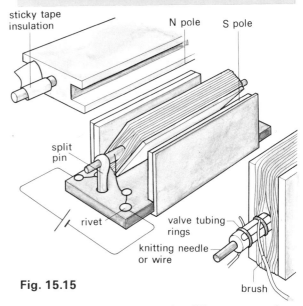

sticky tape
insulation

N pole   S pole

split
pin

rivet   valve tubing
rings

knitting needle
or wire

brush

Fig. 15.15

round. It would just come to rest in an 'up and down' position. But just as it gets into this position the direction of the current in it is changed. This is done by a special kind of rotating switch called a **commutator**. It is connected to the coil by means of springy **brushes**. The side of the coil which at first moved upwards now moves downwards between the magnets, and so the coil is kept spinning.

Connect the motor to a power pack. Before switching on find out what voltage the motor is supposed to work on. Then adjust the power pack to that value and switch on. Watch what happens.

The electric motor, then, changes electrical energy into mechanical or kinetic energy.

Make a list of all the things you can think of which use electric motors. Against each one write down what other means could be used to drive them if electric motors did not exist. There may be some for which there is no alternative.

If your school has an old motor car starter motor have a look at it. You will find that its magnet can be made very strong. How is this done, and why is it necessary?

In most electric motors the armature is made up of a number of different coils, and the commutator is made up of a similar number of sections. Those at opposite sides of the commutator are each connected to a different end of one coil. You will see that such an arrangement makes the motor run much more smoothly than if there were only one coil.

Now that you know what the different parts of an electric motor are, you can make a model of one yourself. Look at Fig. 15.15. The wooden block with the groove on two sides of it is going to be wound with wire. It will form the armature. The short lengths of aluminium tubing at each end of the block form the axle on which the block rotates. One of these pieces of tubing should have a piece of sticky tape (which is an insulating material) wound round it. Cut two thin slices of valve tubing rubber to make two small rubber rings and slide these onto this tube.

Bare about 2 cm of insulation from the end of a coil of PVC-covered copper wire, bend back the bared end as shown, and fix it under the rubber rings. Now wind between 10 and 16 turns of wire tightly in the groove round the block. Cut off the wire, leaving about 2 cm free. Bare this end and bend it back under the rubber rings on the opposite side of the insulated aluminium tube.

Thread a piece of wire (or a knitting needle) through the aluminium tube and through the two split pins, which form bearings, so that the coil on the block can rotate. The bared copper wire loops form the commutator. Two other wires, which should be connected to the + and − terminals of a power pack, form the 'brushes' as in the diagram.

Put the board with its assembled parts between two magnets as shown. The sides of the magnets which attract each other should be facing. Set the power pack to about 6 volts and switch the current on. Once you have set the coil in motion, it will continue to spin. If the motor does not work when you spin the coil one way, try setting it off in the opposite direction.

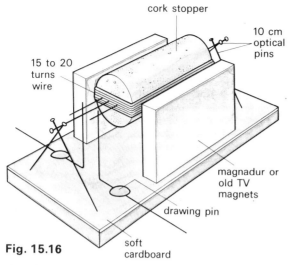

cork stopper

10 cm optical pins

15 to 20 turns wire

magnadur or old TV magnets

drawing pin

soft cardboard

Fig. 15.16

Another way of making a model electric motor from scrap materials is shown in Fig. 15.16. You might be able to make it up at home.

15.11 THE ELECTRICITY SUPPLY

In your electrical experiments you have used batteries of cells, or power packs which were connected to the mains. Where does the electrical energy in the mains supply come from? In the experiment with electric motors, you used electrical energy to make mechanical or movement energy. It ought to be possible to reverse the process and make electrical energy from mechanical energy. This was first done by Michael Faraday in the early part of last century. Try to find out about this very famous scientist from a book in your library. In the next few experiments you will be repeating the kind of work he did, although he did not have such sensitive ammeters as you have. These sensitive meters are called **galvanometers**.

Fig. 15.17 A group of eminent nineteenth century scientists. From left to right: Faraday, Huxley, Wheatstone, Sir David Brewster, and Professor Tyndall. What is each of them famous for?

Experiment 15.12
The dynamo effect or making electrical energy from mechanical energy

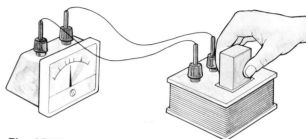

Fig. 15.18

(a) The meter in this experiment is a galvanometer with its pointer set at the middle point of the scale. Move the magnet quickly into the coil. What happens to the pointer? Now move the magnet quickly out of the coil. What happens to the pointer this time? Because the needle kicks from side to side as you move the magnet in and out of the coil, you can say that the current in this coil flows first in one direction and then in the other. This kind of current is called alternating current. You have already used it in Experiment 15.3. Your household electrical supply is alternating current.

(b) Hold the magnet still and move the coil up and down. What happens to the pointer?

(c) Hold the magnet inside the coil and move them both up and down together. Does the pointer change this time? It seems that you only make – or 'induce' – current in the coil when *either* the coil *or* the magnet moves.

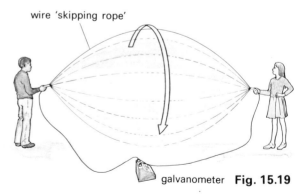

wire 'skipping rope'

galvanometer **Fig. 15.19**

(d) The Earth behaves as if it was a huge magnet. Spin a big skipping rope made of wire flex in the playground. Does the galvanometer needle indicate that any current is flowing?

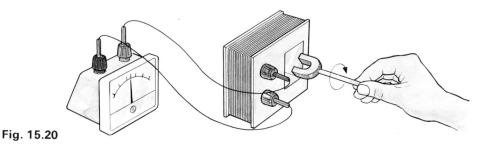

Fig. 15.20

(e) Spin the magnet close to the coil. What kind of current is produced?

(f) **The cycle dynamo**

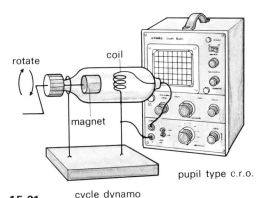

Fig. 15.21 cycle dynamo

pupil type c.r.o.

As you can see from the cut-away diagram of the cycle dynamo (Fig. 15.21), to make the bulb light a magnet has to spin near a coil just as in part (e) of this experiment.

Connect the cycle dynamo to a galvanometer and turn the handle. What kind of current does it make?

Now connect the dynamo to the cathode ray oscilloscope. Ask your teacher to help you with the adjustments. If the 'time base' is switched off what happens to the spot on the screen when you turn the dynamo? What does this mean?

Now switch on the time base. What kind of pattern is made as you drive the dynamo? What does it tell you about the current generated by the dynamo? A dynamo changes movement energy into electrical energy.

(g) **An old motor car dynamo**
Your school may have an old dynamo from a car scrap yard. If you unscrew it and take it to bits, you will find it is rather like a car starter motor. What parts can you recognise?

The large dynamos in power stations are simply much bigger versions of cycle dynamos but they use electro-magnets instead of permanent magnets. (Why?) The dynamos are driven in various ways. Some are powered by water falling from a high level to a low level and passing through turbines. These are called hydro-electric power stations. What kind of countries will be able to generate electrical energy in this way?

In other places, generators are turned by steam turbines in which the steam is raised by burning coal or oil, or by using the heat from a nuclear reactor. In the future, energy from the wind and waves will also play an increasing part in driving generators.

15.12 ELECTRONICS

In Unit 7 (Book 1) you found that some insulators could be charged by rubbing them.

Experiment 15.13
Charges

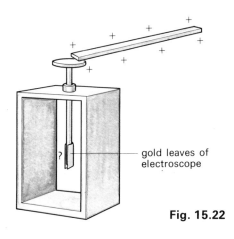

gold leaves of electroscope

Fig. 15.22

Charge a plastic strip and touch it against the cap of an electroscope (Fig. 15.22). What do you see happening to the gold leaves? Why does this happen?

If you have used a charged cellulose acetate strip you will have put positive charges on the cap of the electroscope. These travel down to the leaves and, as both the leaves now have positive charges, they will repel each other.

Now remove the plastic strip and touch the cap of the electroscope with your finger. What happens to the leaves? Why does this happen? Are the positive charges still there? What kind of charges would be needed to cancel them out? These negative charges must have come from somewhere. As you touched the electroscope they may have come from your body. They must in any case have travelled *through* your body to get to the leaves. The negative charges, you will remember, are called **electrons**.

There are several other ways of discharging an electroscope. Try bringing a Bunsen flame near the cap of a charged electroscope. What happens? Where, do you think, have the electrons come from that are necessary to cancel out the positive charges?

It is worthwhile trying out the experiments with the van de Graaff generator that you did in Unit 7 again to remind yourself of them. You will remember that in one experiment thin wooden leaves were fixed to the dome of the generator. When the dome was charged positively one leaf rose, if the air was dry enough. Here is an opportunity to try different methods of discharging the dome.

Experiment 15.14
Cancelling out charges

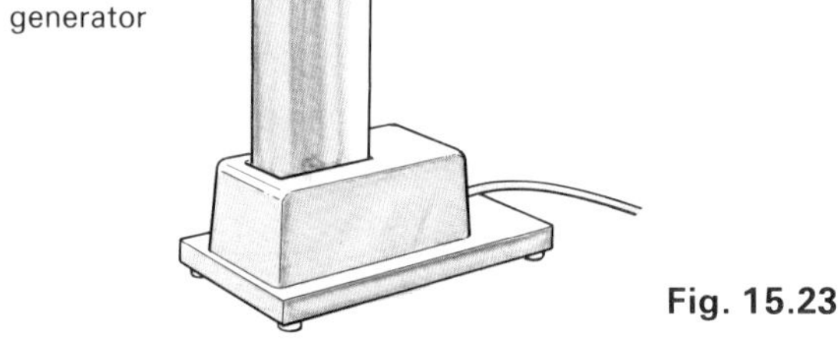

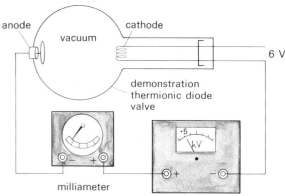

Fig. 15.23

Find out what happens when a heated spiral of wire is held near the dome of the generator (Fig. 15.23). What must the heated wire be giving off in order to cancel out the positive charges on the dome?

These electrons can only have come from the atoms of the wire. Perhaps when the wire is heated the atoms in it vibrate so much that the electrons on the outside of some atoms are flung off, and are attracted by the force due to the positive charges on the dome. The voltage of the dome may be as high as 250 000 volts, so it will certainly have a strong attractive force for electrons.

15.13 ONE-WAY CONDUCTION

Here is another experiment for your teacher to demonstrate.

Fig. 15.24

The circuit shown in Fig. 15.24 is fitted up. The spiral of wire (called the filament) in the evacuated tube gets hot when it is connected to a 6 V supply. What particles will it be giving off? What kind of charges do they have?

When the extra high tension (E.H.T.) supply is switched on, positive charges will be put on to the disc (called the anode) in the tube. Watch what happens to the milliammeter. If it shows a reading you know that a stream of electrons must be passing through it. Trace out the complete circuit in which the electrons are flowing. They must flow from the filament (sometimes called the cathode), through the empty space in the tube to the anode, through the wire to the meter, then to the positive terminal of the E.H.T. unit, and out from the negative terminal to the cathode.

The connection on the E.H.T. unit will now be reversed so that there is a negative charge on the anode. Is there any current flowing through the meter now? Explain what is happening. Remember that like charges repel each other, so that when negative charges are put on the anode they will repel the electrons driven off from the cathode.

Obviously, electrons will flow through this tube in one direction only. They will only flow when the anode is given a positive charge and not when it has a negative charge. Devices which allow flow in one direction only are called valves. There is something like this controlling the flow of air into bicycle tyres: it will allow air to flow in but not out. Similarly, valves prevent the blood in your veins from flowing backwards.

The tube which was used in the last experiment is a kind of electronic **valve**. Because it has two parts, an anode and a cathode, it is called a **diode** valve. Diode valves are used to convert alternating current (i.e. current which flows first one way and then the opposite way) into direct current (i.e. current which flows in one direction only). When an alternating current is converted into a direct one it is said to have been **rectified**. The diode valve can be used as a rectifier. Television sets and mains radio sets contain rectifiers to change the household alternating current into the direct current needed to make the set work properly.

The electrons given off by a hot wire are sometimes called thermions, and this kind of valve is therefore called a thermionic valve. Nowadays the thermionic valve is usually replaced by a transistor.

Experiment 15.15
Transistor diodes

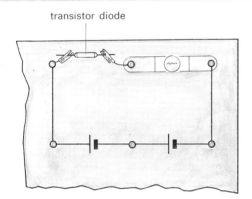

Fig. 15.25

Set up the circuit shown in Fig. 15.25 on your circuit board. What happens to the bulb when you take out the transistor and reverse it in the circuit?

Replace the transistor by a resistor marked with one brown and two black bands. Does the bulb light? If you reverse the resistor in the circuit, does the bulb still light?

You have found that current can flow in either direction through a resistor, but in one direction only through a transistor. So a transistor is a rectifier.

Experiment 15.16
The Maltese cross tube

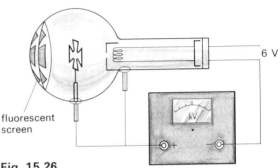

Fig. 15.26

So that you can understand even more clearly what happens in a diode valve, your teacher will set up a circuit using a Maltese cross tube, as shown in Fig. 15.26. This tube is very like a diode. The filament is the cathode and this time the anode is a cylinder. Do you remember what kind of charge must be given to the anode if it is to attract electrons away from the cathode? The cathode is often called an 'electron gun' because electrons are shot off from it.

One end of the tube is painted with a substance which glows when electrons hit it. This is called the screen. Watch what happens on the screen when positive charges are put onto the cross. You will see a shadow on it. What does the shadow look like? You can explain this effect by supposing that electrons shot off from the cathode fly through the anode. If they are stopped by the Maltese cross they cannot reach the screen, which therefore remains black at this point. If, however, they do get by – and they will do this if they do not hit the obstacle – they make the screen glow.

What happens when a strong magnet is brought near the tube? What must be happening to the beam of electrons? Can you suggest another way of getting much the same effect?

Sometimes the electrons flying off the cathode are called 'cathode rays' because the electrons come from the cathode, and they speed along the tube in a straight line, like rays of light. A special version of this kind of tube is used in the cathode ray oscilloscope (c.r.o.) which you have already used in Unit 11. It is also used in a TV tube.

Experiment 15.17
The cathode ray oscilloscope

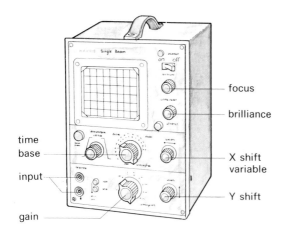

Fig. 15.27

Switch on the oscilloscope. You will have to wait a few seconds before seeing anything on the screen. For your purpose it is best to start with the 'time base' switched off. If after about 10 seconds there is still nothing to be seen, try turning the 'shift' and 'variable' knobs in turn. You should find that when you turn one of them a blob of light appears on the screen. The 'shift' control will move it up or down, and the 'variable' knob will move it from left to right. Try to bring the spot to the centre of the screen. Now adjust the 'brightness' and 'focus' knobs to bring the blob of light to a sharp point and a suitable brightness. What causes the blob of light? Try bringing up a magnet to the screen. What happens? Can you suggest how the 'shift' and 'variable' controls might work?

The tube in the c.r.o. is very like that used in the last experiment. At the back there is an electron gun firing electrons through a hollow anode onto the screen. Switch on the time base to positions 1, 2, and 3 in turn and watch what happens to the spot travelling across the screen.

In a television tube the electrons move across the screen in lines which are very close together – there are 625 lines in the height of the screen.

Connect the output from a power pack (alternating current) to your c.r.o. Use about 4 V. What do you see on the screen? Connect a microphone to the c.r.o. input terminals, and sound a tuning fork in front of it. Can you explain the pattern you see on the screen? Sing or speak into the microphone. What kind of pattern do you get this time? Why is it more complex than the pattern you get with a tuning fork?

15.14 STRIP LIGHTING

Experiment 15.18

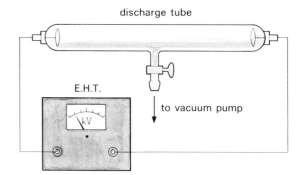

Fig. 15.28

The apparatus needed for this experiment is a long glass tube containing two plates or wires connected to terminals at the end of the tube. The tube can be connected to an air pump which will suck the air out of it. A voltage of 5000 volts is connected across the two terminals from an E.H.T. supply. Does anything happen?

The pump is now started up. Watch what happens as the air is removed. When the pressure gets low enough you will see a violet glow in the tube; this splits up into bands which get further and further apart as the air is taken out of the tube.

The charge on the positive anode is strong enough to pull out electrons from the metal atoms of the negative cathode. If, however, there is air in the tube at ordinary pressure these electrons do not get very far before they collide with molecules of oxygen or nitrogen. When most of the air particles are removed by the pump, the electrons can travel quite a way before they hit one. If the electrons are able to avoid collision with air particles at first, they speed up so much that when they do collide with air particles they have sufficient energy of movement to make the air particles glow. This principle is used in the fluorescent tubes which are often used nowadays for electric lighting and for advertisement signs. In these tubes the gas not only gives out visible light when it is bombarded by electrons in this way, but also invisible ultra-violet light. This ultra-violet light makes substances which are painted on the tube glow.

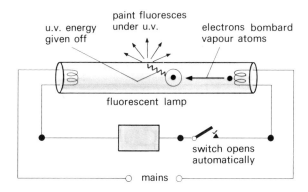

u.v. energy given off
paint fluoresces under u.v.
electrons bombard vapour atoms
fluorescent lamp
switch opens automatically
mains

Fig. 15.29

Because fluorescent tubes are long, they cast very little shadow and are very good at transforming electrical energy into light energy. As you know, the other type of electric lamp has a thin spiral of wire inside it (called the filament) which gets hot when an electric current is passed through it. It is not as efficient as the fluorescent tube because much of the electrical energy is converted into heat (which is often not needed), and only some of it is converted into light energy. A 40 W fluorescent tube can give out as much light as a 100 W filament lamp.

The colour of the light given out by a fluorescent tube depends upon the kind of gas in the tube and upon the substance used to coat the inside of the tube. By choosing these correctly, the light can be made very nearly the same as daylight. The orange-coloured light given out by some street lamps is produced by tubes which have sodium vapour in them – you already know, from your work in Unit 12, that sodium atoms give out a yellow-coloured light when heated. The street lamps which give out a bluish-white light contain mercury vapour. Red, green, and blue advertising signs contain the noble gases.

WHAT YOU HAVE LEARNT IN THIS UNIT

1 The domestic electricity supply is at a much higher voltage than that of an ordinary battery. It is therefore capable of giving you a severe 'shock' and you must take great care not to touch any conductor connected to the mains. All such conductors are protected by a layer of insulating material through which the current cannot pass. This may be made of plastic or rubber.

2 The power of an electrical appliance is the rate at which it uses electrical energy and is measured in joules per second, or watts. To find the power in watts multiply the voltage (volts) by the current taken (amps).

3 The electrical energy that an appliance uses is measured in joules or in kilowatt hours.

1 kilowatt hour = 3 600 000 joules (or 3.6×10^6 joules)

To find the number of kilowatt hours (or units) an appliance uses, multiply the power in kilowatts by the time in hours for which it is used.

4 It is important when choosing fuse wire to select the wire suitable for a current *just* greater than the current which the appliance normally uses.

5 An electric current flowing through a wire coil has a magnetic effect. This effect is stronger when (a) the current is stronger, (b) more turns are used on the coil, and (c) an iron core is put inside the coil.

6 The iron core of an electromagnet is magnetized only while current flows in the coil.

7 When an electric current flows in a wire near a magnet the wire receives a force. This force is used in electric motors.

8 When either a coil of wire or a magnet moves near the other, an electric current is induced in the coil. This current alternates in direction. This effect is used in the **dynamo** and makes it possible to generate electricity by using mechanical energy.

9 Our domestic electricity supply is alternating current (a.c.). Current flows alternately in one direction for 1/100 s and then in the opposite direction for 1/100 s. One cycle of current takes 1/50 s, so that there are 50 cycles of current each second. Our supply has therefore a frequency of 50 Hz.

10 Alternating current can be changed into direct current by a rectifier. Valves and transistors are used as rectifiers.

11 Electrons are given off from heated wires. This is used in the 'electron gun' in cathode ray oscilloscopes and TV tubes.

12 When electrons hit a screen coated with certain chemicals they make the screen glow. This fact is used in TV tubes.

NEW WORDS YOU HAVE MET IN THIS UNIT

alternating current (a.c.)   an electric current which flows first in one direction and then in the opposite direction, usually many times per second.

armature   the moving coil in an electric motor or generator.

brushes   conductors (usually copper or carbon) which lead the current into the armature of a motor or generator through the commutator. They 'brush' against the sections of the commutator as it revolves.

commutator   a switch which can rotate and the sections of which are connected to the coils of the armature of a motor or generator.

direct current (d.c.)   an electric current which flows always in one direction.

galvanometer   a sensitive meter for detecting an electric current.

hertz   the unit of frequency, or the number of times a thing happens in a second.

joule   a unit of energy.

kilowatt hour   the rate of transfer of energy when 1000 watts are converted in one hour. In the case of electricity it is usually referred to as a 'unit' of electricity.

oscilloscope   an instrument for studying variations in voltage in a circuit by making a beam of electrons strike a screen which is thus caused to glow. The movement of the beam corresponds to changes in direction and size of voltage.

rectifier   an appliance for changing alternating current into direct current.

transistor   a material which allows the electric current to flow through it in only one direction.

wattage   the rate at which energy is converted into other forms of energy in an electric circuit. It is also called the power.

SOME QUESTIONS FOR YOU

1   A pupil says that the current flowing in a circuit is 1.5 volts. What is wrong with this statement?

2   A battery has a total voltage of 9 volts. It sends a current of 1.5 A through a resistor. What current would a 12 V battery send through the same resistor?

3   What is meant by saying that the frequency of the electricity mains is 50 hertz?

4   If electricity costs 5p a unit, how much will it cost to run
   (a) a 40 W lamp for 8 hours a day for 30 days;
   (b) a 750 W electric iron for 2 hours;
   (c) a 70 W electric towel rail for 5 hours a day for 14 days;
   (d) a 3000 W immersion heater for 3 hours a day for 100 days;
   (e) a 3 W transistor radio for 5 hours a day for 60 days?

5   All the appliances in question 4 run off 240 V mains. What current will flow through each?

6   Fill in the missing words in these statements.
   (a) An electric motor converts .... energy into .... energy.
   (b) A dynamo converts .... energy into .... energy.
   (c) A diode can be used to .... an alternating current.

Answers

4   (a) 48p   (b) 7.5p   (c) 24.5p   (d) £45   (e) 4.5p
5   (a) 0.16 A   (b) 3.125 A   (c) 0.29 A   (d) 12.5 A   (e) 0.0125 A

Index